REDLINE ARCHEOLOGY

A HISTORY OF DIGGIN' UP ORIGINAL HOT WHEELS COLLECTIONS

Bob Young

Redlines Rock Publishing

Hot Wheels, Redline, Spectraflame, Sizzlers, Flying Colors, and all associated trademarks are registered and owned by Mattel Incorporated and are used in this book solely for identification purposes. Neither the author nor the publisher of this book are sponsored by or associated with Mattel Incorporated. All opinions are those of the author and not of Mattel Incorporated. The cars, race sets, and accessories featured and photographed in this book are from the Bob Young personal collection, owned exclusively by Bob Young. All rights reserved.

The information contained within this book is true and complete to the best of the author's knowledge. Any and all recommendations are made without any guarantee on the part of the author or publisher, who disclaim any liability incurred in connection with the use of the information or any specific details.

Copyright © 2018 Bob Young

All rights reserved.

ISBN-13: 978-0-692-14878-5

ACKNOWLEDGMENTS

To my beautiful and loving wife Deborah, thank you for supporting me in pursuing my passion of diggin' up the original Hot Wheels collections.

To my three amazing children, Madison, Kyle, and Natalie, thank you for understanding and supporting your dad's crazy obsession.

To my parents, George and Betty, thanks for getting me started with Hot Wheels.

To all my true friends who continue to shake their heads, laugh, and wonder what's next. Thanks for all your support, friendship, and shared laughs over the years. Don't worry, something else is just around the corner.

To all the collectors who share the same passion for this wonderful toy car line, thanks for all your support during the many years of witnessing and sharing in all the amazing collections I've been able to unearth.

TABLE OF CONTENTS

INTRODUCTION 7
Chapter One: *The Wonder Years* 8
Chapter Two: *The Indiana Jones in Me* 13
Chapter Three: *And So It Begins* 15
Chapter Four: *The Best Christmas Ever* 18
Chapter Five: *Getting Back To Betty* 26
Chapter Six: *It's All About The Hunt* 28
Chapter Seven: *Don't Count Your Chickens* 32
Chapter Eight: *The Early Discoveries* 37
Chapter Nine: *The Recent Discoveries* 56
Chapter Ten: *My Secrets Revealed* 97
Chapter Eleven: *The Hunt Goes On* 106

INTRODUCTION

It was a beautiful fall day, back in October of 1991, when my phone rang. On the other end of the line was my mother. "Bobby , come to the house and get your, and your brother's old toys out of the attic." I, of course, being of the inquisitive type, asked, "What's the big rush?" She replied, in her typical stern fashion that I never grew accustomed to, even at the ripe old age of 31, "Because I said so, and because we're getting ready to sell the house and move into an over fifty-five community." I was in total shock. Admittedly, I was a little bit upset and heartbroken at the prospect of my childhood home being sold. I also knew that if I didn't get over there in a reasonable amount of time, my cherished childhood memories would be sitting on the front porch, subjected to all the elements. My childhood toys consisted of, first and foremost, my beloved Hot Wheels. I had seventy-two total, plus a lot of Sizzlers and accessories that made some of the best childhood memories. My brother's toys basically consisted of a GI Joe foot locker and some accessories. We didn't have much, but what we had made us very happy back in the '60s.

Needless to say, I drove over to my old house the following Saturday morning only to find my mother already in the attic going through piles of dusty boxes, including my toys. This is where my story gets really interesting. But let's back up a bit and start from the beginning.

CHAPTER ONE

The Wonder Years

The year was 1960. I was born Robert Wendell Young to Elizabeth ("Betty") and George William Young Jr. during the month of July. Well, that's always been an interesting debate in my family, because I was born around midnight on June 30. The doctor told my mother the date of my birth was her choice. She chose July 1 because, "It was an easier date to remember." Either way, it was a typical hot, summer day in South Jersey. Lady of Lourdes Hospital in Camden, NJ seemed to be the popular spot back then for babies being born in the region, and I was no exception. Lots of important people were born on this day, for example; Evelyn Champagne King of Disco Fame with hits like, SHAME and I'M IN LOVE. Also, many important historical events took place. Like, GHANA gaining their independence; Neale Fraser defeated Rod Laver at Wimbledon, and Status Indians gained the right to vote in Canada. These all pale in comparison to the release of Etch-A-Sketch by The Ohio Art Company. I must confess, I missed it by eleven days, but I was pretty darn close.

I spent the first fifteen months of my life in a small town named Woodbury Heights, New Jersey. It was only five minutes from work for my father at the Texaco Eagle Point Plant Refinery located in Westville. My parents eventually wanted to move into a new home and community, and, along with my older brother and sister, they settled on Stratford, New Jersey in the fall of 1961. Stratford was a small, blue collar community, where most men carried a lunch pail and thermos to work each day. Rarely did I ever witness one of the dads wearing a suit or tie. Stratford is located about twenty minutes east of Philadelphia and about an hour's ride to the Jersey Shore. The Jersey Shore was where, if you were lucky enough, the family vacationed for one week in July or August. I truly only remember a couple of family vacations during my childhood spent there. The other vacations were typically spent around my hometown of

Stratford, doing what most children did at the time, swimming, fishing, stickball, etc.. We didn't know any differently, and these were truly the best of times.

Back in the '60s, things were very structured in my community. Our family sat down to dinner every night and the grandparents typically joined us for dinner every Sunday. We only spoke if spoken to, and addressed our elders by Mister or Misses. We all had to attend Sunday School, in a suit and tie of course, and a full church service afterwards. It was a bit tortuous for a young boy back then to have to sit and basically not move or squirm for three straight hours, but I managed. Following the service, as soon as we finished shaking the pastor's hand, all the kids were shot out of a cannon in a full sprint to their respective cars. Ties were being pulled on to loosen them, at the same time you were ripping your suit jacket off, trying to win the race to your parent's car. It was a real thing back then and I'm sure many of you can relate to this.

Other than the regular scuffle I had with my older brother, my childhood was nothing less than amazing. Growing up with modest means really didn't impact my childhood, other than I probably would have had well over 500 Hot Wheels and every race set ever produced, if I had come from a privileged environment. I feel pretty confident about that, because I asked for literally every car, race set, and accessory that Mattel produced while growing up.

I, along with all my friends, enjoyed the freedoms that the sixties provided. Getting up at the crack of dawn on weekends, packing a brown bag lunch loaded with Twinkies and TASTYKAKES, and heading out for a day filled with , street hockey, running in the woods, and riding bikes all over the neighborhood, was very typical. If you stayed inside and didn't come out to play, you were looked upon negatively. Most parents wouldn't allow any of us to stay inside, even if the weather was not so inviting. Both my parents developed a very convincing death stare, if we were inside for too long on the weekend.

The only time during the day on the weekends that we ever heard from either parent was dinner time. My father had a voice that was unrivalled in the neighborhood. Everyone knew George's voice. My father was a strapping six feet, one inch in height, a former high school athlete, World War II decorated Veteran, and oil refinery union worker for 35 years. When he called us for dinner, we either ran as fast as we could, or pedaled very quickly and without hesitation. We never wanted to be late for dinner in my family. My mother, on the other hand, was a towering five foot two inches tall, but don't let size fool you. Betty could swing a wooden spoon and yard stick better than the Babe. So when that call came in, back in the fall of 1991, to come and get my toys out of the attic, I listened very intently, took notes, and acted accordingly. I didn't want to make history as the first thirty one year old to get a beating with a wooden spoon.

My sister was eight years older than me and really only paid attention to me early on in my life. I was kind of like a real live baby doll that was at her disposal. She did however, unknowingly , buy me the greatest Christmas present of all time. We'll revisit this later. My brother on the other hand, oh boy did we have a tumultuous shared youth. We fought just about every time our paths crossed. It was so bad, that when my parents wanted to have a night out, they had to hire two babysitters, one for me and one for my brother. Even my grandparents refused to babysit us following their one and only experience with my brother and me. When I turned sixteen, I grew ten inches. So in 1976, he learned a very hard and painful lesson to never take liberties on my face, head, or body again. It was the final fight. Ali and Frasier had nothing on us. Unfortunately for my parents, they didn't go out much during our childhood.

Some of my fonder memories growing up are of times spent collecting newspapers and magazines so that my dad could take them into Camden and get five cents a pound. I would jump on my little Schwinn and scour the neighborhood the day before trash day, grabbing as much paper as I could. I was only four years old, to the best of my memory, when this all began for me. Twelve inch bundles of paper, floor to ceiling, tied with string, engulfed our garage until the end of each month. Then we loaded up the trunk and back seat in my dad's Oldsmobile, and headed into Camden. My dad took full advantage of free labor, me and my brother, to earn some extra, much needed cash for the family, and his beer. We typically would have to take at least three to four trips on any given Saturday to deliver all the paper we had collected over the previous month. The overstuffed back end of the family car would scrape on the road every time we hit a bump on the way to the paper plant. A lot of the time I would have to sit on a bundle of paper in the backseat because there was no room for me anywhere. My brother and I never saw a penny of the money earned, but understood, even at a very early age, the family's need and we were happy to do it. Well, most of the time anyway.

Throughout my childhood, my mother always described me as a leader. Whatever I was into at the time, the neighborhood kids were into as well. It drove a lot of the parents crazy over the years, so I was told. I turned out to be quite a hustler, always looking to make money. Looking back, I was a natural born entrepreneur and businessman. I had a paper route, ran mini-carnivals off my front porch, owned a tropical fish breeding business out of my parents garage, shoveled snow, mowed lawns, babysat, captured snakes that got into the neighbors gardens, performed magic shows, and, well, you get the point. My older brother would even hustle his friends on the block into playing his baby brother (Me) in tabletop hockey. I had a natural gift at playing this oh so fun game, and my brother seized the opportunity. It was one of the few times during my childhood that I can remember my brother being a little bit civil to me. He would hustle his friends in to thinking they would beat this skinny little five year old at the game we all enjoyed. The bets were always a dime per game because that's what got you a fresh pack of baseball cards at the local, general store. I think the best part of those packs of baseball cards was the pink, flat, powdered piece of stale gum that came inside. At least it was for this kid. In the end, I beat all his friends handily in every game I played, but they quickly figured out the hustle. Looking back, my brother probably only made a few bucks because I got fifty percent of the take, but that was huge back in the '60s.

The most interesting part of my entrepreneurial background as a child was the tropical fish business. Back in the winter of 1972 was when my first business homerun was hit. I just didn't realize it until much later in life. So this is how the story goes. Initially, I had to convince my parents to allow me to convert our one car garage into my dream of owning a tropical fish store. I maintained a twenty gallon fish tank for years and loved every minute of it. My parents finally agreed, under two conditions: 1. I had to pay to have the extra electrical line put in, and 2. I had to pay my parents four dollars a month towards the electric bill. I agreed instantly and got to work. The electric line installation cost me eleven dollars. That was my entire take from my twelfth birthday that year. Oh well, I was committed and gladly paid the electrician. I was off to the races. I trash picked old carpet to cover the cement floor. I trash picked refrigerators and gutted them, plugged up the holes in the shell with acrylic gel, and turned them upside down to use as breeding tanks for fancy guppies and other live bearers. I would go around and collect old two by fours to build shelves to hold some of my tanks. Neighbors would donate old fish tanks to me that they no longer needed. I hustled and got the word out and some people really were excited for me. I would go to the library and read up on how to breed tropical fish, live bearers and egg layers. I was totally committed, or should have been committed some will still tell you to this day. I called my new business venture the "FISH HUT" and hung a handmade, multi-marker, colored cardboard sign on our lamp post for all to see. The weather never cooperated, so every few weeks I had to make a new sign. It was New Jersey after all. The neighbors started coming by to check out what Bobby Young was up to now. By the end of the fall of 1972, I was averaging forty dollars a week selling all kinds of fish that I had successfully bred. That kind of money back then was unheard of, especially for a twelve year old. Most school teachers barely earned that kind of money. I was selling to neighbors from Stratford mainly, but word had gotten out to other surrounding towns as well. I started selling to local pet stores and out of towners. It was truly unbelievable, and I had a hard time keeping up with the demand. My prices were so good that they couldn't get enough, especially the pet store owners. I even employed some of the girls on the block to sweep the floors, feed the fish, change the filters, and basically keep the place looking good. There was a schedule and sign-in sheet I created and placed on the wall for my employees. I paid 10 cents an hour and everyone was happy. Hard to believe , but all true, and I learned a ton from that small business of mine.

The business became so well known that it actually caught the attention of the zoning office in town. My parents were eventually paid a visit by the zoning officer in Stratford and told that they either apply for a variance to designate their property as commercial, or shut down the business. I would have loved to have been a fly on the wall when this conversation took place. It just had to bring a smile to both my parents' faces. There was no way my parents were going to fill out the paperwork and pay the money necessary. But the fact that my business was that successful must have made them proud. I don't think I need to say much more, except that all my stock and inventory was sold over the next two weeks, and the "FISH HUT" was now just a memory. One heck of a memory, but still a memory. My next homerun in business, unfortunately, would have to wait another 25 years.

CHAPTER TWO

The Indiana Jones in Me

Aside from all my business ventures and a fostered entrepreneurial spirit, I was a typical boy growing up in a typical post war town. I played baseball, ice hockey, fished, and just enjoyed my youth immensely in the '60s and '70s. But my true passion was digging up old things. I remember riding my bike to Parkview Elementary School, the place I spent years 5 through 11, and bringing my mother's garden spade along. I would just pick a spot at random in the school yard, and start digging. Not sure of what I was going to find, I just had the desire to unearth things, anything. One day, to my surprise and amazement, it finally happened. I actually uncovered something of value. After weeks of only finding cool rocks, which I littered my little desk at home with, I came across something historic. I dug up not one, not two, but three Indian arrowheads. I jumped onto my bike and pedaled as fast as I could to show my mother just what her amazing, amateur archaeologist discovered. She was actually impressed with what was laid on the kitchen table before her. Now I was really motivated to dig up more treasures. I went on to uncover old Indian pottery, spearheads, and other artifacts that were verified at the local library by a town historian. We were informed that where I was digging, was actually an old Lenni Lenape Indian campsite along the Signey Run River. The river had since dried up, and was now just a tiny, trickling creek due to all the development now surrounding it. From that point on, I was hooked and knew that I wanted to become an archaeologist.

My passion and desire to uncover and discover pretty much anything, certainly did not end with the Indian campsite finds. There was an old dump that I discovered, along with one of my friends and his father, in the neighboring town of Laurel Springs. Looking back on that experience, the dump had to be well over 100 years old because of the markings and colors of the items we pulled out of the ground. Everything from lite blue, blue, green, and red medicinal bottles, pewter and silverware, plates, bowls and just about anything else they would have tossed out at the time. My garage, which had recently housed the "FISH HUT," was now a storage unit for all my new discoveries. My parents weren't very happy and eventually threw everything out one weekend when I was away at a friend's house. I still wonder what all that old stuff would have been worth nowadays. I, to this day, never understood why they threw it all away. It was just the way it was, and I had no choice but to accept it and move on. It's probably how I developed my high level of patience over the years.

Undeterred, my passion for discovery continued into my young adulthood. Even though my parents knew my dream was to go to college and study archeology, they shut me down immediately. They explained that I would never be able to support myself as an archaeologist, digging up old dinosaur bones and the like. I, of course, didn't challenge them, and went on to college and pursued other careers. But my desire to become an archaeologist never wavered. Today, and for the past 25 years, I continue to scratch my archaeology itch by digging up vintage, original, one owner Hot Wheels collections from all over the country. For me, it's two fold. For starters, my passion to uncover and discover hidden treasures. Secondly, my love of one of the most important toys made. The ingenuity and overall "Fun" factor makes the entire line of Hot Wheels, truly the greatest boy's toy ever made. Mattel consistently introduced more and more amazing accessories and new car models that kept my interest piqued for years. In my opinion, there is no toy in the world cooler than the original Redline Hot Wheels.

CHAPTER THREE

And So it Begins

I remember the day like it was yesterday, July 1, 1968. A day that is etched in my mind forever. It was a typical hot and humid day in New Jersey, and my birthday celebration would once again be held on a picnic table at the Stratford Swim Club. This was the hot spot for throwing children's birthday parties back in the day, and what every parent could afford, because it didn't cost a cent. Always a special day for me, and one I looked forward to each year, because I always received some cool toys from my friends. I had all my best friends in attendance, Paul, Bobby C., Jeff, John, Joe, and Andre. The presents were piled up on the picnic table and I just couldn't wait to rip into them. The day of swimming, eating hot dogs, playing shuffle board, horseshoes, and just plain horsing around came to an exciting end when my mother herded us like cattle back to the picnic table to sing Happy Birthday. As soon as the final words of the song were belted out by my band of heathens (friends), I started ripping through my presents like a hungry wolf eats its prey.

My friends, and of course their parents, didn't disappoint as I received some very memorable and cool gifts. I still remember a Captain Action figure with a parachute, a large Superball (most baby boomers know the distinction), the board game, Operation, and a Johnny West doll with his trusted horse and camping gear. It was a really good day for me and I couldn't believe the generosity of my friends. I know what you are thinking. What about the Hot Wheels? The best was yet to come, but it would have to wait until I got home.

The party ended, we said our goodbyes, packed up the family car, the blue, four door Chevy Bel-Air, and headed back home to the family celebration of my oh so important birthday. At least that's what I was thinking. As soon as we got home, my mother got right to it, making dinner for the entire family like she did every day. My beloved grandparents showed up shortly thereafter, and it was game time. Dinner was served, and for basically the only day of the year, I was the center of attention. I soaked it all up and couldn't wait for my so-called BIG present, which in reality wasn't that big, but a kid could dream, right? We all finished our dinner, and as usual, patiently waited for my sweet grandmother Katherine, Mam-Mom as we called her, to finish her meal. She, to this day, holds the Guinness Book of World Records for the most meticulous and slowest eater on the planet. She was the sweetest woman I ever met, and I miss her dearly.

Finally, the table was cleared and out came my birthday cake ablaze with a whopping eight candles. No need back then to call the fire department like today when my birthday cakes are brought out. My family sang the traditional song and my grandmother planted a big, wet, post dinner kiss on my left cheek that I feverishly wiped off like most eight year olds would have done. Out marched my mother, who placed three presents on the dinner table right in front of me. One from my grandparents, one from my parents, and of course, one from my brother and sister that I'm sure was bought and wrapped by my mother. I started with my brother and sister's present, because I always wanted to save the best for last. I attacked it like the house was on fire, ripping through the thick decorative paper and mounds of scotch tape. It was a Spirograph, and I was thrilled. For me, art , next to physical education and lunchtime, was my favorite class . Next up was the gift from my grandparents. It was a tall, rectangular shaped box and that only peaked my interest even more. I got right to it and ripped it open just as aggressively as the previous gift. It was a toy like no other. A medieval knights and castle small action figure set, reminiscent of the dark, green army men that were highlighted in the movie Toy Story. But instead, it had silver and gold, little, plastic knights, with horses and two plastic castles for each side. A war game that encompassed catapults, rock throwers, drawbridges, and archers. I would eventually spend many a rainy day playing with this unique toy with my friends, and we loved it. Catapults would go crashing into our enemy's castle with archers and knights flying everywhere. Draw bridges were knocked off their bearings and the castle would begin to fall, one section at a time, with every thunderous catapult and rock strike, and victory was within my grasp.

The time was finally upon me. The BIG gift time from my parents. Little did I know, that the next two minutes of my life would be a defining moment for me, even at the ripe old age of eight. My mother walked back in with my last gift, a very long, thin, rectangular shaped box, with another oddly shaped gift taped to it. I remember relishing the moment, as it appeared that I was getting not one toy, but two. The anticipation was killing me and I began tearing the paper from the larger of the two. Once the paper was completely pulled off, absolutely the coolest looking gift I had received up to that point in my life was revealed. The colors on the long skinny box were incredible. The art work was unlike anything I had ever seen. Not like I took many, if any, trips to the toy store. But still, I had never laid eyes on anything like it before. None of my friends had it, nor had I ever seen any advertisements for something called a Hot Wheels STRIP ACTION SET by Mattel. I still was a bit unsure what to do with it until I opened the smaller present attached to it. At that very moment, I laid eyes on my very first Hot Wheel, a blue with black roof, dark interior Custom Camaro with a collector's button. The packaging, the art work, and just the overall look put me into a state of pure awe. Truly the first time I ever fell in love, well, toy love that is.

I just couldn't wait to figure this oh so complicated toy out. I was also surprised to find a blue Custom Firebird inside the race set. My level of excitement was through the roof. I quickly read the brief yet succinct instructions, and in no time, I was running my new found loves down the ten feet of orange track. I quickly called my friends on the phone and invited them over to witness the greatest boy's toy ever made. Something as simple as placing a plastic, purple clamp on a table, and attaching orange track that was held together by, of course, purple connectors, was simply unparalleled. Ironically, orange and purple were always my favorite colors, so it truly was a match made in Hot Wheels' heaven.

Now, I was on a mission to collect the other 14 cars pictured on the side of the box. My mother worked part-time at a JC Penney's store nearby in Audubon, New Jersey. She worked every Friday night, and due to the fact that we only had one family car at the time, my father and I would go pick her up at the end of her shift. I would stay in the car while my dad went in or we would just meet her out in front of the store. However, I soon figured out that JC Penney's had a toy department, and from my 8th birthday forward, I somehow convinced my father to take me inside with him. The toy department was located on the second floor, and we had to walk right past it on the way to meet my mom. I was in heaven. My first time there I feverishly searched out the section where the newly released line of Hot Wheels and all the glorious race sets and accessories were on display. I can still see the end cap and pegs with all the sweet sixteen cars proudly displayed. It left an indelible mark on my memory. I would go on to visit nirvana (JC Penney toy department) every Friday night religiously for the next four years. This was just the beginning of a life-long love affair and obsession with this most ingenious line of toys created by Mattel.

CHAPTER FOUR

The Best Christmas Ever

As with most children, Christmas for me was the most magical time of the year. My birthday was a close second, but there was just something about Christmas that not only brought out the best in people, but was also responsible for a great toy or two under the tree each year for us. Even as a child, I understood the true meaning of the holiday, but still enjoyed the fact that I got to open presents the morning of. It was a special time that was very important to my family and community.

My oh so very important Christmas list for Santa Claus in 1968, I'm sure, pretty much only contained Hot Wheels. The cars were listed by model and color, which was always either purple or orange, in addition to every race set and accessory Mattel had produced up to that point. I would leaf through the JC Penney catalog that my mother would bring home before the holidays and check off every Hot Wheels item and add each one to my ever growing Christmas list. However, Christmas at the Young household was also an opportunity for my mother to give me and my brother what she called the "essentials." What this meant, was that every year, year after year, my brother and I would receive the same and most uninteresting gifts under the tree. You can say a lot of things about my parents, but they certainly were consistent. The essentials were a three pack of JC Penney briefs with my name tag sewn into the back of the elastic band on each, a three pack of JC Penney undershirts again with the name tags sewn in, a pair of JC Penney jeans, and a pair of Jeepers. Jeepers were the cheap, and I mean cheap version of Chuck Taylors back in the day.

Now that you are starting to get a snapshot of what my Christmas looked like, it wasn't all boring. I knew that my parents would come through with a few goodies. They did the best they could with what they had. I also knew that my aunts and grandmother would come through with a cool toy or two. Christmas morning 1968 finally arrived, and I dashed down the steps, barely coming into contact with anything but the bannister and the first floor. I rushed over to open my presents and all I could hear was this booming, deep voice coming from the second floor proclaiming "Do not open any of your presents until your brother and sister wake up." Well, if they weren't awake prior to that boisterous command, they certainly were then. So as I always did, I listened to my parents and waited very impatiently for my brother and sister to make their way downstairs. It felt like an eternity, but I'm sure it was only a few minutes. In that short waiting period, I was carefully examining each and every one of my presents and had figured out what 90 percent of them were, even still wrapped up in their glory.

All bets were off now. As soon as we got the green light from my parents, we all started in on ripping our presents open. Earlier in the year my dad had purchased an eight millimeter home video camera, that, when the four lights on it were given juice, Apollo 13 could have used our house as a marker to get home. I was half blinded while opening my gifts, but that didn't slow me down in the least. I had gotten through the obligatory essentials, and yes, they all had my name sewn into them once again. You could always count on Betty. Next up after the essentials, was the stocking. Being asthmatic, the doctor always told me and my parents that I was never to have milk, chocolate, or peanuts. Needless to say, my stocking was always void of any good candy, and bubble gum typically took center stage. I almost forgot to mention the stocking essentials which were the annual toothbrush and toothpaste. Once I finished unwrapping my final piece of Bazooka bubble gum from my stocking, it was show time. The time when, after strategically opening all the boring stuff, it was time to open the real good stuff. First up was a box that you would normally put a dress shirt in. I ripped off the paper, lifted the top of the cardboard box lid and boom, there they were, four Hot Wheels' cars in all their glory. A green Hot Heap, a lime green Silhouette, a purple Custom T-Bird, and a lime green Custom Mustang. These cars were so important to me, that even to this day, I could still tell you every car I owned as a child, and its color. I'm sure some of you can relate. This is a true testament to the impact this line of toys had and still has on me to this day, even as an adult.

Next up were the two that I predicted would be the crown jewels of my Christmas 1968. I was right in my assessment and they didn't disappoint. The first was a package about two feet long, six inches high, and weighed about a pound or two. It was a Hot Wheels Stunt Action Set with an orange Beatnik Bandit in the window. I was so excited to get the car out and set up the track that I practically forgot about the last present that looked identical to the first. I took a deep breath, and even if I tried, could not have wiped the Cheshire cat smile off my face as I opened my last present under the tree. I started to get a little light headed when I realized it was a Hot Wheels Drag-Race Action Set. This set had a starting gate and finish-line so I could actually race my cars and enjoy some friendly competition with my friends. Yes, Christmas 1968, was one for the record books.

When 1969 rolled around it was another year filled with Hot Wheels joy. My parents realized how much enjoyment my friends and I garnered from these little gems and decided that, as long as I was a good boy, there was a chance that, on Friday nights, I could actually pick out a car when picking my mother up from work. I was a good kid the majority of the time. At least this is what I was told by my mother and father later in life. So as the story goes, I picked up a new car nearly every Friday night during that year. My collection now required not only a 24-car case, but also a 48-car case to house my ever growing stable of Hot Wheels. My parents realized this and both cases were given to me on my birthday that year. I also received a bunch of cars and accessories for my birthday that same year from my friends and relatives. My collection was growing at a rate that I couldn't have ever dreamed of, and I was thrilled.

Christmas 1969 rolled around and, even with my high expectations, some things never change. I was, once again, blinded by my father's 8mm flood lights while opening my presents. And yes, Betty came through with the personalized underwear and undershirts, JC Penney jeans, and of course, Jeepers. The anticipation was just as great as it was the previous year but this year was different I actually unwrapped some size D batteries in my stocking. Thinking to myself, why in the world does my mother now think I need batteries, and what use could I possibly have for them? My questions were answered soon thereafter when I opened the Hot Wheels Super Charger Race Set with a red Python and blue Custom Cougar in the window. I think I momentarily lost consciousness due to the overwhelming nature of this new, ingenious creation by Mattel. I must've gone through dozens of batteries over time playing with this incredible invention. It was truly ground breaking for the time and one of the most popular race sets that I can remember amongst all my friends. We all seemed to have at least one Super Charger as part of our collections. Some of my friends ended up with the two directional, two story Super Chargers that totally blew my mind.

The icing on the cake that year was the Hot Wheels Double Dare Race Action Set which housed a Red Custom Camaro and Aqua Custom Barracuda. Just another great addition to my already incredible collection. Christmas 1969 came and went and left me with some great lifelong joyous memories, and my Hot Wheels were at the center of it all.

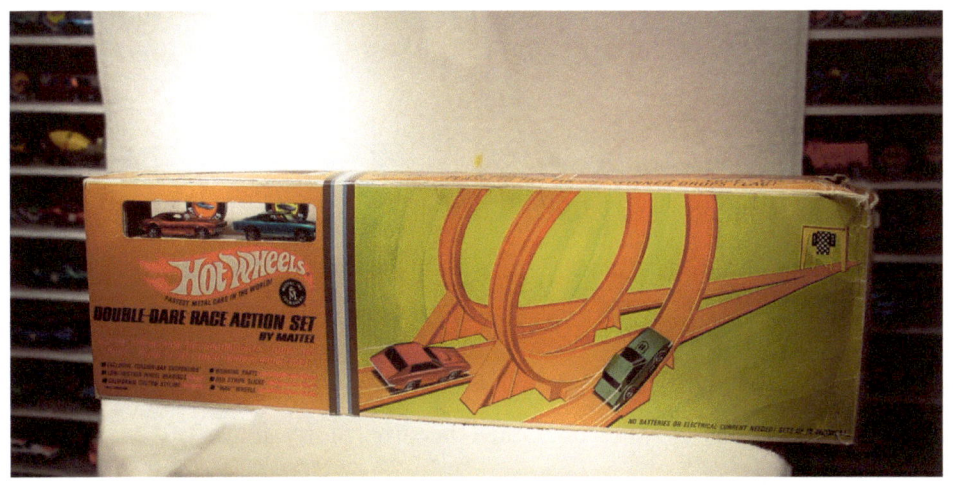

My Double-Dare Race Action Set from Christmas 1969

My Double-Dare Race Action Set from Christmas 1969

1970 was a year very similar to the previous, but it was the year I always look back on as one of the greatest in my childhood. I was still allowed to occasionally pick out a car on some Friday nights as my parents slowed my roll down a bit. My 10th birthday also was par for the course with bolstering my collection and adding a few more very cool accessories like the Dual Lane Speedometer, Dual Lane Lap Counter, Rod Runner, and Trestle Five Pak. I immediately incorporated all of these new accessories in my track lay-outs. The track lay-outs were becoming more and more elaborate and somewhat obnoxious over time, sometimes even spanning two floors in our house. My friends and I became pretty ingenious with our designs, and they were certainly well thought out. Well, most of the time anyway. We literally would spend hours racing, stunting, and even timing the cars. It was way too much fun, but we soaked it in as much as we could.

Trestle Five Pak Birthday 1970

1970 was also special to me and my family for another reason. I was awarded the MVP in Stratford Little League. This was an honor that only two athletes per age group were awarded each year, and my name actually made it into the local paper. My parents were thrilled and I was some type of urban legend that summer around town. Looking back on it now, I guess it was my 15 minutes of fame. Even though I understood how much of a big deal it was to be named MVP, what happened during Christmas, for me, was unquestionably my greatest moment of 1970.

Christmas finally rolled around and it was basically the same ole story. I was blinded, once again, by an eight millimeter camera and opened all the essentials that were personalized just for me. I cleared out my bubble gum riddled stocking that also contained my annual toothbrush and toothpaste wrapped like a real present. I eventually got around to opening the good stuff. My sister had just graduated from high school in the spring of 1970 and accepted a good paying job in Philadelphia for a major law firm as one of the partners' administrative assistants. She was still living at home and paying rent, but she had good cash flow that I finally realized upon opening her gift to me that year. My sister's gift was square shaped, a little over a foot tall and a foot wide, and weighed approximately two pounds. I had dreamt about owning this ever since laying eyes on it at JC Penney, but I was so excited that I just didn't put two and two together. It was the first time that I didn't have any clue as to what I was getting. I got right to it as soon as I exchanged presents with her, and to my surprise, it was the hallowed Hot Wheels TUNE UP Tower. Ahhhhhhhhhhhhhhhhh, the clouds separated, the sun peeked through, and I felt the glorious warmth that it produced. The angels came down from heaven and were singing, enjoying this most incredible moment with me. I was so happy that I think I actually shed a tear or two. I just literally couldn't believe my eyes. I gave my sister the most heart felt hug I had ever given anyone in my life up to this point.

My original Tune Up Tower

I wasted zero time in carefully taking all the pieces out of the box and reading the instructions. Momentarily, I thought about asking my father to help me with the assembly, but I could already hear his voice in my head telling me to do it myself, so I avoided the disappointment and started the assembly process.

Assembly of the TUNE UP Tower was now complete and it was time to show it off. I called all my friends to come on over, bring their Hot Wheels, and check out my new addition. Oddly enough, I was the only one of my friends to ever own a TUNE UP Tower, which really made it that much more special to me. Once again, I cannot imagine how many D size batteries I must have blown through over the next two years playing with this incredible toy. Watching the cars enter the elevator, ascend to the second and third floors, and ultimately get tested on the Dyno Meter was a thing of marvel. I would test each and every one of my cars and make sure that all their alignments and axles were perfect. The intuitive, little, tune-up tool that was included was truly a masterpiece. The Hot Wheels line of toys were so well thought out and constructed, that rarely did anything ever go wrong with any of the moving parts that couldn't be easily remedied, even by a ten year old. Christmas 1970 was truly my greatest Christmas ever and I give all the credit to my sister. Thanks sis!

CHAPTER FIVE

Getting Back to Betty

My childhood years came and went, but the joy that came from Hot Wheels never left me. My mother always did realize just how important the cars and everything that went along with them were to me. I played with my Hot Wheels regularly until 1972. The reason I know this is because I ended up with a Funny Money from that year in my collection. Other things in my life gained my interest, especially playing ice hockey. The Philadelphia Flyers, over the next few years ended up winning two Stanley Cups, and that was all the distraction I would need. Then girls came along, and, well, that explains the next several years.

Returning to that fateful Saturday morning in October 1991, while back at my old, childhood house to pick up my old toys, was a day like most days. A very typical fall day in the northeast with a crisp cool bite in the air and falling leaves littered the lawns, sidewalks, and streets. I made my way up the stairs to the second floor, and there was my mother, backing up, tail-end first, out of the attic. The door to the attic was only three foot tall and approximately two feet wide. It wasn't an easy orifice to navigate at any age. First thing my mother said to me after mumbling a muffled, "Hi Bobby," was, "Get your and your brother's toys out of the house or I will." I knew what that meant for sure. It meant that if I didn't do exactly what was asked of me right then and there, my cherished childhood toys would have found their way to the local Goodwill store, or worse yet, the trash can. Mom didn't play around and always meant what she said.

I rushed past her as soon as she finished backing out of the attic and started grabbing the boxes I recognized first. There was dust everywhere, including the inside of each of my nostrils and both of my eyes. It was not a pleasant experience, but I knew it had to be done right then and there. This was my one and only chance to rescue my cherished toys from the grasp of Betty. I packed up all the boxes, both mine and my brother's which included, Captain Action, Johnny West and his horse, GI Joe and his foot locker full of goodies, all of my Hot Wheels and accessories, the strange Castle game, Operation board game, Which Witch board game, Spirograph, Incredible Edibles, Mouse Trap game, and others. I sincerely thanked my mother for saving all of my childhood toys and she told me that she knew how much I enjoyed them growing up as the reason why she held onto them. I loaded up my Pathfinder and I was off.

Upon arriving back home with all the toys, I emptied out my car and took the entire lot down to the basement, where in my mind, I thought they belonged. I placed all the boxes in a corner and that's where they stayed for the next few weeks. When I finally got around to going through them, wow, did that stir up some really good feelings and memories. The smells, oh the smells. All the different toys still had the same unique smell to them and that was the single most factor that started to stir up my childhood memories and emotions. There they were, in all their glory, my beloved Hot Wheels. My most cherished, childhood toy was now in front of me and my nose, and boy were all my senses stimulated. Opening each of the car cases for the first time in over twenty years was a very emotional moment for me. The look, the smell, and the overall feeling was a bit overwhelming at some level. I think I actually shed a tear of joy, immense joy in seeing my long lost friends after all these years. I almost felt bad that I had left them abandoned in the dusty old attic at my childhood home for all those years. I kind of felt guilty in a weird way, but I was so happy that they were finally home where they belonged, with me.

My oldest daughter Madison was a little over two years old at the time and was curious, just like any toddler would be, while looking at my old toys. She got into my Hot Wheels one day and started to play with them. By playing with them, I mean throwing them around the basement and stuffing them between the couch cushions. I eventually got around to showing her how the cars were truly meant to be played with, and set up a track so she could experience the cars the way I did back in the '60s and '70s. Her attention span wasn't at a point where she actually sat for more than 10 seconds to watch dear old dad play with his old toys, but it was fun nonetheless. She eventually lost interest within the first five minutes, so we were on to other things like playing with dolls or going to the park. My cars were still strewn all over the basement, but I really didn't think that they had much value at the time, until Betty brought something to my attention. And that was where a new chapter in my life all began.

CHAPTER SIX

It's All About the Hunt

It had been about eighteen months since I rounded up my old toys from my parent's attic when my mother showed up to my house for a short visit like she typically would. She had brought with her a newspaper clipping that she wanted to share with me. My mom was an avid reader her whole life and never missed any local, regional, or national news. This was no exception, and she handed me a small article out of the local newspaper that covered the Delaware Valley, including the Philadelphia region. The article was titled, "Mattel prepares to celebrate Hot Wheels 25th Anniversary." The article went on to discuss the worldwide success that Hot Wheels had enjoyed over the past two and a half decades. It went on to mention that the 69 cent toys from 1968 may now have some real value due to a booming collector base. I was in shock while reading this and couldn't believe that these little cars, that barely cost a buck back in the day, may have some significant value amongst collectors. I immediately gave thought to my cars and panicked, because I knew they were out of the cases, littered all over our basement.

I ran down the basement stairs and started to carefully gather them all up and place them back in their safe haven, the cases. I then carried them up to my office, locking the door behind me. I actually found them in the toy box, under the couch, between the couch cushions, lying in the middle of the basement floor, and every other nook and cranny a two-year old seems to discover. The cars were then safe, so I immediately started to research online to see if I could get any information on what exactly my cars were worth. Back then, dial up AOL was about our only choice in a server. I can still hear the dial up sounds that went along with jumping online with AOL. It was a very unique series of noises that most of us from this generation would recognize to this day.

I eventually came across a Hot Wheels message board and chat room online, so I went ahead and joined in the conversation. As soon as I introduced myself and stated what I had, all hell broke loose. I couldn't believe the response I received from all the collectors, so I just sat back and soaked it all in. One of the first questions was whether my collection contained an OLDS 442. Of course it did, as I had pretty much every car produced during my childhood years. When I replied affirmative and started to describe my collection, nearly everyone in the chat room and message board started to private message me wanting to buy my collection along with all the accessories. I wasn't anywhere near ready to sell my beloved Hot Wheels, but I knew that this was something that needed a lot more exploration and research on my part.

The following day I went to Borders Bookstore and purchased a collectors guide for Hot Wheels that one of the online members recommended. I started leafing through it and could not believe my eyes as I re-read the car values listed in the book, especially for my OLDS 442. I took a couple of weeks to digest the information that I was getting online and in the guide. I needed some time to wrap my head around what my next step was going to be. My collection was very special and sacred to me in a way that only someone my age, who loved the cars as I did, would understand. I got to thinking that, if I still had all my Hot Wheels cars and accessories, there must be a lot of other people my age that still had the stuff stored away as well.

The entrepreneur in me started to stir once again. I also started to ponder about how to get the word out that I was a self-proclaimed Hot Wheels collector of the original cars from the '60s and '70s. I jumped in head first, as I always did with all my business ventures, and started to come up with ideas on how to market to my targets. My target market was anyone at the time born between the years 1956 to 1966. I figured I'd capture the majority of the individuals that were of the age that would have played with the cars back then. It certainly was not an exact science, but at least it was a starting point.

My goal was to test the market with some simple flyers that I created on my computer and start by posting them on supermarket bulletin boards, retirement villages and over fifty-five's community boards, and any local business that had a dedicated area that was open to flyers or business cards. I tried this approach for about a month before I moved onto Plan B. Plan B was designing and ordering 500 business cards that said, "I Buy Old Toys," in the center with Hot Wheels and Johnny Lightnings written underneath it. I also added, "Top Dollar Paid," with a bunch of dollar signs beneath it in the bottom left corner of the card. I, of course added my contact information in the bottom right corner. The best part was the graphic of a Corvette that was at the top middle of the card. It was direct and right to the point. Individuals who had Hot Wheels would certainly understand why I added Johnny Lightnings to the card as most of us had some scattered throughout our collections.

The original business card I designed

I passed out the business cards to all my friends and anyone I ran into that even looked close to my age. Between the flyers and business cards, I scored a total of zero collections in the first couple of months. Frustration was beginning to set in and I knew that I needed to change it up a bit. I finally decided, after not receiving one call over the first three months, that I would probably have to spend some real money on marketing if I were to dig up any collections locally. I just didn't know where I needed to spend the money.

One day I was reading a local newspaper's sport's section, like I did pretty frequently, and just happened to look at the classified ad section to see if there was anything interesting for sale. I was bored and just thought I'd do some window shopping per se. As I was going through the ads looking at all the cool sports cars, boats, and other interesting items, I stumbled across a section titled "WANTED TO BUY." This was it, the golden ticket I thought to myself, and immediately started reading the ads in the section. Most of the ads were looking for antiques, cars, boats, and homes. I continued going down the list and came across one classified ad that stated that they were looking to buy old toys. This was the best chance I thought that I had to possibly acquire an old Hot Wheels collection. Now I was tasked with calling the newspaper's classified ad section to find out all the details and what this was potentially going to cost me. I was shocked at how expensive it was for a two- line, seven-day classified ad to be run in the WANTED TO BUY section. Back then, $111.00 was a lot of money for me to spend on a simple, classified ad that only ran for a week.

I thought about it for a day or two but made the decision to spend the money. I ran the following ad: I buy old Hot Wheels from the 60's + 70's Top $ Paid phone #. That was it, the magic formula to scoring some old Hot Wheels, so I thought. I called, placed the ad, and I must admit that I did cringe just a little when I gave them payment through my credit card. The day came when the ad went live for the first time. It was a Monday morning in September, 1993, and I remember it well. Monday came and went without a single call, but I kept my chin up and told myself that Tuesday was going to be better. Tuesday arrived with anticipation, but ended up just as disappointing as the previous day. The rest of the week, Wednesday, Thursday, Friday, and Saturday were the same old story, nothing, absolutely nothing. Sunday was the largest circulation day for the newspaper and my last hope. I told myself that if I didn't get a single call from seven days of running the ad, I would pull the ad, never to be run again. The expense at that time was just too great for me and my family, especially if I was getting nothing in return.

Sunday morning came and went, and the same was true for the afternoon hours. I was quickly losing hope and started to think of other possible ways of getting the word out there. Regardless of how the classified ad performed, I was not giving up this easy. I sat down to dinner with my family and our newest addition, our beautiful son Kyle. I looked at Kyle and thought to myself that he will certainly be the heir to my Hot Wheels collection. That was the best I could do as far as Hot Wheels were concerned at the time. Until the phone rang, THE PHONE RANG! On the other end of the line was a woman that quickly asked, "Do you buy the old Hot Wheels?" My heart was now beating a hundred miles a minute, my mouth got dry, and I started to shake a bit. I couldn't believe it, someone actually called and could possibly have an old collection of my favorite toy. I tried to compose myself the best I could and nervously answered, "YES." The next words that came out of her mouth changed my life dramatically. "Great, because I have a case of them and just come and get 'em." I think every thought in my head had left at that very moment, except for one, that this could be my first original childhood Hot Wheels collection discovered. I finally re-gained my composure and discussed the details of the collection with the woman. It sounded like the real deal. A 24- car case full of 1968 and 1969 models. Once this information was confirmed, we discussed a meeting time and location. She offered to meet me at her home address in Woodbury, NJ the next day around noon. Monday felt like a year away. I don't think I slept more than an hour total that night. Little did I realize that this was just the beginning of a long and exciting hunt that would last decades.

CHAPTER SEVEN

Don't Count your Chickens

My excitement grew with every passing second at the mere thought that a collection was within my grasp. Monday morning was upon me, the day that would change my life forever and pull me into the vortex of collecting the old Redline Hot Wheels. At the time, I worked as the athletic trainer for a large high school and wasn't required to be at work until mid-afternoon. This meant I had plenty of time to get to Woodbury and possibly pick up my first collection. Woodbury was only a short thirty minute drive from my house, so I planned on leaving around 11:20 to give myself some extra time, just in case Murphy's Law decided to have some fun with me that day. My first stop was to the ATM to get a few hundred dollars out. I basically emptied my checking account, but I didn't hesitate. Never thinking that I didn't have enough funds to pay for the collection, but what did I know at this point. This was a whole new world I was entering into and didn't know what to expect. I jumped onto the highway that would get me to her address the quickest. I arrived a few minutes early and the woman was sitting in a chair on her front porch with the original 24-car case on her lap. The exact one that I owned from 1968. I could spot that case from a mile away if I had to.

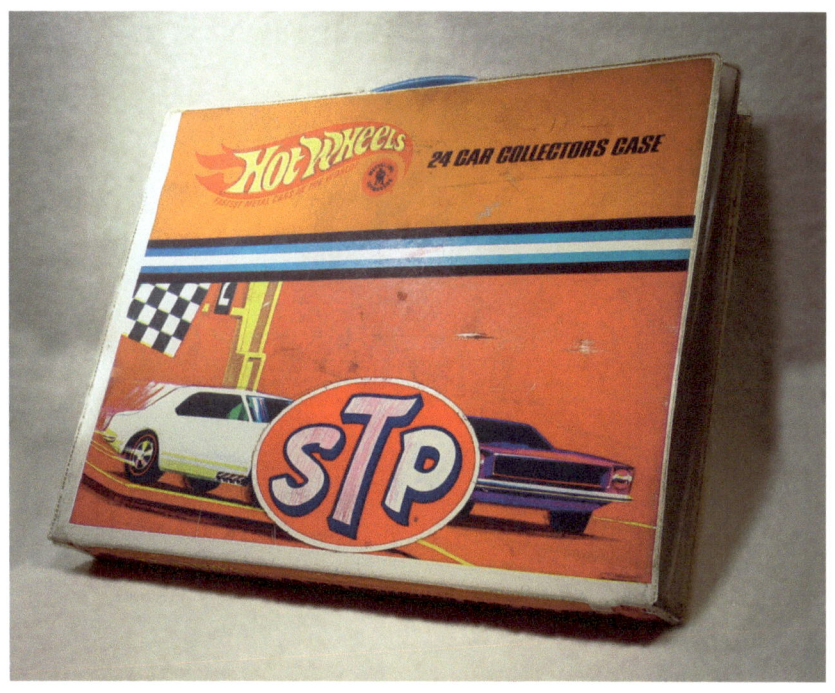

The first collection I dug up back in 1993 from Woodbury, NJ

I walked up and introduced myself to the nice woman and she just handed me the case and said in a Jersey kind of way and a stern look upon her face, "Here, just take these and get them out of here." I was a bit stunned and probably stuttered a bit when I asked her how much she wanted for them. I hadn't even opened the case, nor looked at one car at this point, but I could feel that the case was full and the sound that echoed when she passed the case of cars to me confirmed that there were a lot of smiles in that case. The woman responded to my question with, "I only paid a buck a piece for them when I bought them for my son and he doesn't want them, so just give me two bucks a car." I took a step back and told the woman that I wanted to look at the cars and pay her fairly, as some may be quite valuable these days. She appeared a bit shocked and a certain calmness came over her as she smiled slightly. I proceeded to open the case and it hit me, the distinct smell of the cars and the case. It's a smell that still resonates with my senses to this day when I come across a collection of old Hot Wheels. The collection was mainly '68s with a handful of '69 models. Basically, the cars were in somewhat played with condition, but there were a handful of customs in nice shape. Mainly common colors to each casting, but I ended up paying 250 dollars for the collection, and she was more than happy.

Thankfully the phone rang that fateful Sunday in September,1993, because if it hadn't, there wouldn't be a book to write. I decided to run the same ad again in the Courier-Post until the end of November. I figured most people wouldn't be interested in selling their old toys after that because of the upcoming holiday season. Well, I was not only right in regards to December, but I also didn't receive another phone call in October or November. Now I was out over 1000 dollars in classified ad fees and it didn't feel good. I counted my chickens before they hatched basically. I was convinced that I would be scoring, at minimum, one to two collections a week. Guess what? I was wrong and now needed to come up with a new strategy to acquire collections. By the end of November I regretfully cancelled the classified ad, but it was more a matter of economics at the time and Christmas was upon us. My kid's toys had taken priority and my wife and I were on a strict budget at this time in our lives.

A typical collection I discovered in the 90's

Christmas and New Year's came and went, but I was still pondering my next move in marketing to basically shake the weeds and score more collections. I thought long and hard about where we lived and when would be the best time to start my next campaign. Being from the northeastern part of the country, New Jersey, we all do spring cleaning. It's just part of the culture when old man winter leaves and the warm sun once again shines. Garages are emptied, basements are cleaned out, windows and screens are cleaned, and attics are organized. Yard and garage sales pop up everywhere during this time of year. This all commences sometime in April, typically after Easter, depending on where it falls in any particular year. Then it dawned on me that I could run the classified ad again, but delay it until mid-April. I thought that maybe I could cut some people off at the pass before they laid their old Hot Wheels out for a yard sale. April 1994 rolled around and I went ahead and placed the ad again in the Courier Post newspaper. Unfortunately, April came and went without a single call. I was becoming a bit frustrated but knew that I could go one of two ways. Either I throw in the towel and stop the bleeding, or I double down and roll the dice. I chose the latter approach and went for it.

The Philadelphia Inquirer, at the time, was a local newspaper serving the greater Philadelphia region with a circulation approximately four times greater than the Courier-Post, but was more expensive in the classified ad department. The month of May was upon me and I was starting to feel my potential window of opportunity closing quickly. I had to make a move if I was to continue my pursuit of these elusive cars. I pulled the trigger and placed the exact same ad in the Philadelphia Inquirer's classified ad section as well as the Courier Post's, on Monday, May 2,1994. I remember the date well because, as soon as the ad in the Inquirer went live, my phone started to ring off the hook. And it didn't stop for the entire month. I started to score collection after collection from all over the Delaware Valley. A lot of the collections were coming from the City of Philadelphia in all the older neighborhoods. The ad in the Inquirer was a game changer, and I let it ride through June of that year. The one in the Courier-Post was dead, completely dead. Something unexpected occurred that spring as well. It seemed that, as soon as the calendar flipped into June, the phone almost immediately stopped ringing. It was bizarre, but it seemed to happen every year moving forward from there on out. I eventually learned that my biggest return on investment was the month of May, and only May.

Some of my earliest finds in the 90's

I decided to end the ad running in the Courier-Post moving forward and focused all my efforts and resources on the ad in the Philadelphia Inquirer. I decided to run the ad in the fall to see if there was any magic left with the ad during that time of year. I just figured that it wasn't holiday season, everyone was back from summer vacations, and the kids were back in school, so what the heck and gave it a try. The ad performed poorly in the fall of 1994. Now my sights were solely focused on May of 1995. It felt like an eternity, but I knew that the rest of the year was only draining my bank account and I had given the ad enough time to prove me otherwise. Spring time 1995 was upon me, and boy it did not disappoint in the least. The amount of collections over the next five years were mind blowing, to say the least. I just couldn't believe that this stuff still existed at the level I was buying, but also in the original packaging, which totally blew my mind. All I knew was that, when I was a kid in the '60s and '70s and my parents bought me a new Hot Wheels car, it took a total of five seconds or less for me to rip it out of its plastic bubble. I never understood how in the world they survived unopened for the past two and a half decades. To this day, when I score a collection of all unopened individual Hot Wheels cars, known as Blister Packs in the collector world, I still just shake my head in disbelief. With a smile on my face of course.

CHAPTER EIGHT

The Early Discoveries

I consider the years between 1995 and 2002, to be the glory days of my collecting history. This was a time right before eBay hit, became vastly popular, and ultimately changed my approach to collecting. We'll get back to this later. Let's get to the good stuff, the collections and the stories that accompany them. Although there were many original childhood collections I scored over the first ten years of collecting, I'm going to highlight the most interesting collections in detail.

The Jersey Shore collection

It was a rainy, windy day in New Jersey, May, 1996. My phone rang in response to the classified ad that I was now religiously running the whole month of May each year in the Philadelphia Inquirer. The caller promptly asked, "Are you the guy that buys the old Hot Wheels?" I proudly answered, "Yes I am." She went on to tell me that her ex-husband had left behind his old Hot Wheels and she just wanted them out of her house. She further explained that they had been there over five years and she repeatedly had asked him to come and pick them up. As a common practice for me now, I asked the woman to turn some of the cars over and tell me the name of a few of the vehicles. She proceeded and named many cars from the first three years of production. It was confirmed that this collection was the real deal so we decided on a day and time to meet the following weekend. The collection was located in a small coastal town in New

Jersey called Mystic Island, about a one hour drive for me.

I arrived on time, as always, and was greeted with a very brief, business-like introduction and invited in. The collection, contained in a 24-car flat car case, was sitting on the coffee table in her living room. Once again, it was the exact first case I owned back in the '60s to store my cars. Upon opening the case, I never expected much more than a couple dozen cars. I also expected them to be worn from being played with, in common castings (models) and common colors. I typically set my expectations low to avoid being disappointed at some level. To my surprise, the collection was one for the ages. It contained cars in, not only un-played with, pristine condition, but some cars to this day, I've failed to find in the hundreds of collections I've uncovered, and rarely have seen come up for sale or trade anywhere. The cars appeared as if they were just pulled from the factory line.

Mattel produced cars in bulk due to demand, and the demand for the most part was great. Certain colors of certain castings are rare, very rare, and to find them at all is a miraculous feat. Finding rare cars in mint condition is almost unheard of. I gazed upon the whole collection and had to rub both of my eyes repeatedly to make sure I was seeing what my eyes and brain were telling me. For starters, there were mainly cars from the first year of production, 1968. This is a very good thing as most of those cars are widely sought after by collectors, especially the customs. I don't know how the individual initially found these cars on the peg back in '68, but I still scratch my head to this day thinking about what this collection yielded.

Contained within the collection and in mint, beautiful condition, without a mark, nick, scratch, or any discoloration (toning) to the paint, were the following cars; purple with black roof Custom Cougar, gold Custom Camaro with a white interior, light blue Custom Corvette with white interior, hot pink Custom Eldorado with white interior, orange and purple Custom Mustang with white interior, purple Custom T-Bird, magenta Custom VW, and a hot pink Python with a white interior. There was also a screaming ice blue Mod Quad which I had never seen before. The rest of the cars were in just as impressive condition, but weren't nearly as rare. Thankfully I had brought enough money to make the deal and we both parted ways very happy. The Jersey Shore was always a magical place growing up as a kid and it certainly didn't disappoint on this special day.

Ice Blue Mod Quad discovered in Jersey Shore collection

The Northeast Philly collection

The Northeast Philly collection was one of my favorites early on, and inspired a story that I wrote for a couple of fanzines in the hobby back in the day, including a popular one by the name of "BlisterPak" for their summer 1997 issue. Here's how it went on that beautiful spring day…..

It's a day that I'll never forget, May 1,1997. It started out like any other day in the Young family, wake up, feed the kids, cup of java, get the kids off to school and get ready for work. A typical day until the phone rang at 8:27am. Back then we still had land-lines and this was the number I used in my classified ad. On the other end of the phone was a gentleman who said that he had a collection of old Hot Wheels from the sixties and seventies and was I interested in buying them. I was always skeptical with these calls because, as time went on, nine out of ten calls never amounted to anything. This call however, was different, and I could feel it in my bones. I proceeded to ask the usual questions that would typically vet out each collection to let me know if it was worth the trip into the city or elsewhere. First, I asked him to turn a few of the cars upside down and tell me the names of each individual car that was stamped on the bottom. He started to name a few of the Heavyweights (a line of work vehicles) and some castings from 1973, so I knew this was a legitimate collection. He went on to describe the case that the cars were sitting in and it ended up sounding exactly like the flat forty eight car case that I owned as a kid. I figured that there would be a few decent pieces in the case and it was well worth the trip for me to take a look. I was headed to the Phillies game versus the LA Dodgers that day at Veterans Stadium with my son, so it made sense for me to go a little bit early and check out the collection.

I loaded my son in the car and we were off. We decided to meet earlier in the morning due to his work schedule. I arrived at his home with my son in tow and he welcomed me into his Northeast Philly row home. He directed me to his dining room where he told me the case of Hot Wheels was that we had discussed. I walked into his dining room and gazed upon an eight foot table that was completely covered with cases of Hot Wheels. Not one case, not two, but eight cases of original Hot Wheels cars in all their glory. The cars were not only way more than I expected, but the majority of them were un-played with. A truly amazing sight that I had not seen before. I started the task of going through the cases examining each and every car. I must admit that, at the time, it was pretty hard not to show my cards and maintain some level of decorum. There were seventy castings, seventy three enamels, customs, spoilers, pinks, purples, and blister packs. You name it, it was in there. All from the early years of production and I just couldn't believe what I was seeing.

Naturally I was concerned whether or not I had enough cash on hand and more importantly in my bank account. I wasn't making much money back then and only had access to limited funds. As always, I asked the owner how much they wanted for the entire collection. It was always a good starting point that most people understood and typically already had a figure in mind. He came back with his answer, "I just want them out of my house, they're taking up too much room." I almost collapsed right there on his dining room floor. I momentarily lost consciousness, but quickly regained my composure. I proceeded to empty my pockets giving him every last dime that I had on me, and he accepted graciously. Looking back, I didn't pay nearly enough for the collection only because I didn't have it to give. Fortunately, the gentleman was thrilled that I was getting it all out of his house. It felt like I was basically, in my opinion, doing him a favor at some level.

The owner of the collection went on to tell me the background of the collection which finally put things together for me. He said that the collection was passed down to him from his aunt after his uncle had passed. He went on to say that his uncle would never let him or any of his siblings or cousins play with the cars. It now made perfect sense to me as to why the cars were in such great un-played with condition. The only thing on the cars was twenty eight years of dust.

We shook on the deal and the money exchanged hands. The deal was done and now in the books. All I needed to do was to stay alive long enough to get this phenomenal collection home safely. My heart was pounding out of my chest with excitement. I loaded my son in the car and all eight cases of Hot Wheels while smiling from ear to ear the entire time. I jumped in the front seat and started the car, when I just happen to glance back at the house. I saw the gentleman walking out of the garage with two large, dark green plastic trash bags in each hand and they looked quite stuffed and heavy. Ironically, sticking out of the top of one of the bags was a few pieces of the infamous orange track. My jaw dropped and I thought could this possibly get any better? I put the car in park and shut off the engine. Calmly, as best I could, I exited the car and asked the gentleman what was in the bag. He replied, "Just track and stuff." I asked what he was doing with it and he said it was going out with the trash. I asked if I could have it and he gladly said, "Sure, take it."

When I got home, I opened each of the trash bags and not only found a ton of track and loose accessories, but also discovered many mint in box items that were never opened. I did go to the store that day and buy some lottery tickets, but my numbers didn't hit. I guess my luck had run out.

Blister Pak fanzine Summer '97 issue

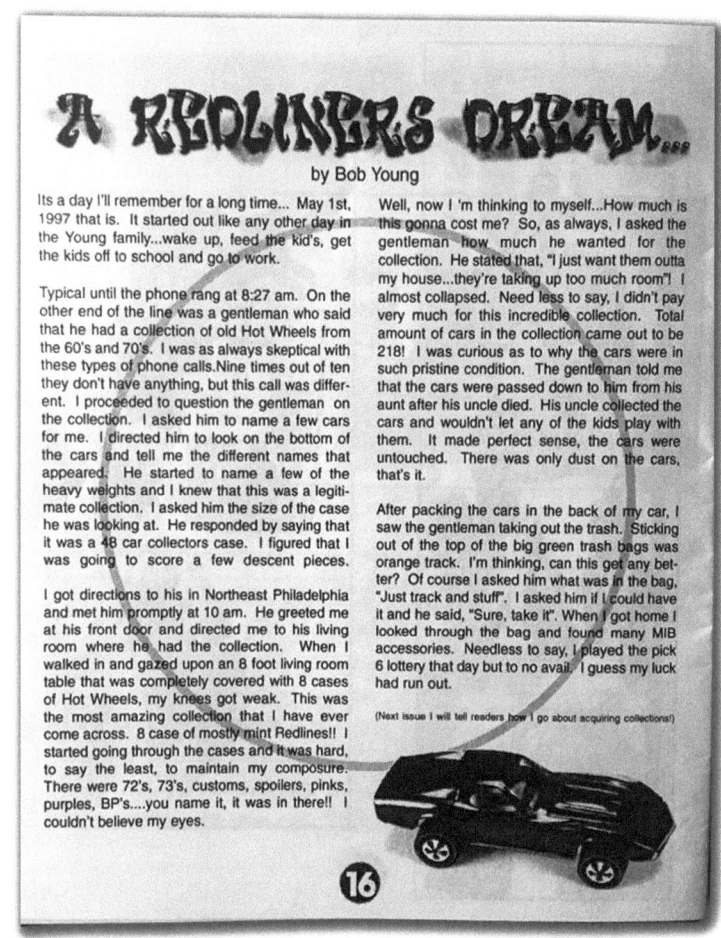

Original article on the Northeast Philly collection

The Leisuretowne Collection

In the spring of 1998, I was contacted by one of the local news station reporters for Channel six Action News in Philadelphia. She introduced herself and asked me if I was the collector of Matchbox cars. I chuckled, then went on to correct her with what I really collected. She laughed, apologized and got right to it. She asked if she could do a human interest story on me for their next broadcast at six o'clock that night. I guess they needed a filler if they were calling me, right?

I didn't understand at the time why the most watched local news station in the city would want to waste any air time on me and my hobby. I asked the reporter this exact question and she stated that each month she goes through the classified ad section in the Philadelphia Inquirer and searches out the most unique and interesting ads that may appeal to viewers. She obviously was impressed by my two line ad. Oh well, even a blind squirrel finds a nut sometimes. I just happened to be the nut this time.

The reporter was on my doorstop within the hour with a cameraman and Channel Six Action News Van. The neighbors probably thought something serious had happened. I set them straight later after the reporter and cameraman had left, and we all had a chuckle or two when the story ran that night at six. The exposure made my phone ring, only once, but it brought in a more than memorable collection anyway. On the other end of the phone was an elderly woman that, once again, asked if I was that Hot Wheels collector, but this time, "the Hot Wheels collector that was on TV last night." I felt somewhat famous for that brief moment and then finally came to my senses. She continued, telling me that she had her two sons' Hot Wheels collection and they were obviously grown and out of the house. Neither of the sons wanted any of the cars or sets and instructed their mother to sell them. She saw the piece on the news and contacted the news station and asked for my number. Thankfully they passed my information on to the woman.

We planned to meet the following morning at her home before I had to be at work. She actually lived in the same over fifty five development that my parents moved to. Ironic that I could possibly score a collection in the same neighborhood that the two people responsible for my addiction now lived. I drove over and met her as she was waiting for me on her front porch, rocking slowly, in her weathered white, rocking chair. A large case of cars sat on her lap and she was flanked by two large boxes on either side. I changed it up a bit and, instead of going after the treasure right away, I decided to save the best for last, the cars. First, I asked her what was in the two boxes sitting next to her and did they have anything to do with Hot Wheels. Sometimes people that called me with collections would also show me old toys and other collectibles that they assumed would be of interest to me. Every once in a while some old Star Wars toys and action figures would show up as well as GI Joe and other toys from the '50s, '60s, and '70s. I never claimed to be an old toy expert and most of the time I would either pass on the other items or call one of my local collector friends to see if they had any interest.

She began opening the first large box and out jumped a Sizzlers Fat Track, power pit, and its beat up box. There were also some loose speedometers, rod runners, and lap counters but that was about it. The next box would prove to be the better of the two, by far. We moved past the first box and opened the second box which contained the good stuff. There was a complete in-the-box Sky Show Set and Road Trials Set and an unopened, near perfect Hot Wheels Club Kit. The Road Trials Set was always my favorite because it contained the Tune Up Tower. I was so thrilled that she wanted all of this to go with the case of cars that still quietly sat on her lap.

Now it was time to get to the Piece de Resistance, the cars of course. She opened the case and once again, I was astonished and totally blown away by what was in front of me. I didn't even bother rubbing my eyes this time as every collection by now I learned was unique in its own way. I never get used to seeing a collection like this, but I have learned over time to maintain my composure for personal health reasons. Her two sons must have each loved one color and one color only. Although the two colors were different, boy did they have good taste when it came to Hot Wheels.

In the case were 48 of the most magnificent purple and blue Hot Wheels I have ever laid eyes on. 24 purple and exactly 24 blue. The only way this collection could've been any better was if one of the sons loved the color orange, but I'll take it nonetheless. Some of the highlights of this collection were a blue Openfire, purple Custom Camaro, Custom Mustang, and Custom Cougar, lite blue Python, Custom Corvette, and Carabo. It seemed that, back then, it didn't matter much what shade of blue it was. Also, magenta seemed to work if purple in a certain casting couldn't be located on the pegs in the stores, and this collection was no exception. A few magentas were scattered amongst the purples as well and they were; Custom Eldorado with white interior, Custom VW with white interior, Hot Heap, and an Evil Weevil.

All in all, this was truly a memorable collection that I actually have the local six o'clock news to thank for. As the saying goes in business, any exposure is good exposure. Not sure if I truly believe that wholeheartedly, but certainly it applied in this case.

Some of the original cars from the Leisuretowne collection

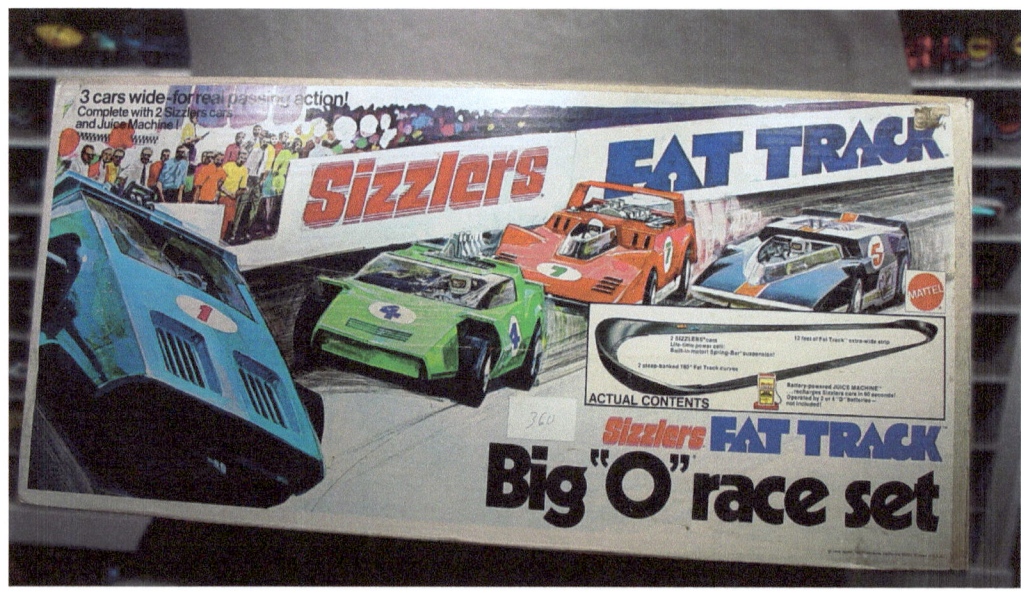

Original Fat Track from the Leisuretowne collection

Elkins Park collection

The year 2000 came and went, and a new dawn was upon us. It was two years later in the spring of 2002, when one car in a massive collection made it all worthwhile. My classified ad had already been running for 4 weeks, and it was approaching the end of May when every year it was pulled. It was on the last day of my ad running, June second to be exact, that my phone once again rang with a woman on the other end asking the same question as always, "Do you buy the old Hot Wheels?" "Of course" I answered. She answered all my preliminary questions perfectly, so I was once again assured that there was some pot of gold at the end of this rainbow. We met that Sunday evening at her home in Elkins Park, Pennsylvania.

I took my collector friend Todd with me on this run like I had many times before. Todd loved watching the deals go down and seeing the cars being dusted off as much as I did. We knocked on the door and all I heard was a voice coming from somewhere in the house directing us to "Come on in, the door's open." Following orders, we proceeded through the front screened-in porch and into the main house. Upon entering the tiny, ranch style home, it was shocking to say the least. Thinking back on it now, it reminded me of an episode of Hoarders. We could barely find a path to walk through single file, and I remember wondering what we were doing there and if we were going to make it out alive. It was a bit uncomfortable at the onset, but we were quickly greeted by the owner who put our minds at ease almost immediately with her smile and calm demeanor. She explained that she had boxes of the old Hot Wheels in her back room and needed some help bringing them out. Like forging a path in an overgrown rain forest, Todd and I eventually made it twenty feet into the kitchen where there were two cardboard boxes with multiple Matchbox and Hot Wheels cases stacked on top of each other. Todd and I started to rummage through the cases and it was a bit disappointing, but we kept at it. All in all there were about fifty played with Hot Wheels from the early days, lots of worthless Matchbox cars, and one Johnny Lightning.

For me, growing up, there was nothing that compared to my Hot Wheels. The Matchbox cars that I would receive every once in a while from some relative or friend, couldn't even make it to the end of a ten foot track. Johnny Lightnings were cool but were a little too 'over the top' for me and looked like they were from another planet outside of our galaxy. They just didn't have the appeal or fun factor like the Hot Wheels delivered on a consistent basis. The designers at Mattel, back in the early days of Hot Wheels, were so ingenious with what they produced. The race sets and all the amazing accessories were way ahead of their time. Super Chargers, Rod Runners, Tune Up Towers, opening parachutes, loops, Sizzlers, Fat Track, and the list just goes on and on. I loved everything they came up with and would have owned them all in a perfect world. To me as a young kid of the '60s, my jaw dropped every time I found something new on the shelves at the toy store when it had to do with Hot Wheels.

I made the deal with the nice lady and Todd and I packed up the cars and were on our way. It wasn't until the next day when another one of my collector friends, John, stopped by to see my latest score that the bombshell was dropped. John was not only a huge Hot Wheels collector, but he was just as obsessed and very knowledgeable regarding the original Johnny Lightning cars and sets. He took one look at the Johnny Lightning car that was part of the collection, stared at me and said, "Do you know what you have here?" I, of course, replied in my curt, Jersey style, "Yes John, it's a Johnny Lightning. More specifically, I even know that it's a Custom GTO." The car just happened to be hot pink metallic which I found out that day was the most desirable color according to Johnny Lightning collectors, especially for this particular casting.

John also went on to say something about the wheel wells being painted, a possible indication that the car might have been a salesman's prototype instead of a regular production run. John looked the car over and immediately offered me 2000 dollars. I told John thank you for the generous offer but I needed to hold onto the car for a couple of weeks before I let it go. I typically would do this so I could learn as much as I could from fellow collectors about the cars I had just uncovered. It was a good rule to follow and has always served me well, even to this day. John understood and said he would get back to me in a couple of weeks. He called me the next day and almost every day after that trying to pry that car from my clenched fist. I stuck to my guns and held onto it.

There was an upcoming East Coast Redliners meeting taking place the following weekend, so I decided to load up all my most recent finds along with this mysterious hot pink metallic Custom GTO and my glass display case to see what deals could be had. The meetings were always a great time and drew collectors from Virginia to Connecticut and everywhere in between. The East Coast Redliners was a group of Hot Wheels collectors that concentrated on the first ten years of production. The meeting this time was on a Sunday in North Jersey at a local car dealership that one of the members worked at and was granted permission to use the facility. I placed around fifty of my newest finds, including blister packs, all along my table and the more rare pieces under lock and key in my glass table top display case. Todd was with me so we shared the table. There were some pretty well-known collectors in attendance, and one in particular that had a lot of interest in the Johnny Lightning pink Custom GTO.

To cut to the chase, the GTO was confirmed by many knowledgeable collectors in attendance to, in fact, be a salesman's prototype. It was also in mint, loose condition to boot. After about an hour or two of negotiating, I ended up trading the GTO for two mint, in blister packs, Olds 442's, one blue and one green. It was the greatest trade to date in my collecting career. Considering what I paid for the car as part of a decent sized collection, I was way ahead on the value meter. Both of us were extremely happy with the deal, and who knows, maybe that car today has more value on the market than my two Olds 442 blister packs, but I don't care. I would still do that deal without hesitation to this day. Hot Wheels always win in my book!

The original Johnny Lightning Hot Pink Custom GTO Salesman's Prototype

Original green OLDS 442 Blister Pack

The Crème de la Crème Partie Un

The Tacony Collection

    As always, I try to save the best and most memorable find from my early days of collecting for last. The story I'm about to tell is true, and only the names have been changed to protect the innocent. Dragnet was one of my favorite shows, just saying. It was a cold and rainy day on this thirteenth day of May, 2003. A day that I certainly will never forget in a million years and one that may have to be etched on my tombstone.

    The call came in early in the morning, early enough to wake me and my family. On the other end of the phone was an older gentleman that asked the obvious question I was always asked, "Are you the guy that collects the old Hot Wheels?" I answered affirmatively and went on with my scripted questions that I had certainly memorized by now. The gentleman was a bit closed-lipped when answering my questions, but satisfied me enough to make the trip over the Tacony-Palmyra bridge and into the Tacony neighborhood of Philadelphia. Tacony is a small, historic neighborhood located about eight miles north of downtown or center city Philadelphia. Everything checked out for the most part, in my mind, so we planned on meeting later that morning as per his request. I remember that he was in a bit of a jam and needed for me to meet with him as soon as possible. I obliged and I was off to the city. He lived in a very old neighborhood in what was still a decent part of the city. His home was what we call a brownstone and was in the middle of the block. He told me he would save me his parking spot right in front of his house. He was a man of his word. I found the address and out front of his house in the street, curb side, was a lawn chair. To this day, this is common practice in Philadelphia when reserving your precious parking spots. I beeped the horn as he instructed, and he waddled carefully down the slick steps with umbrella in hand and removed the chair. I relied on my parallel parking skills and pulled into the tight spot after only two tries.

I proceeded to walk up the steps to his front door and was welcomed inside. The house was built in a way that it set up about a half story which allowed a full basement to be contained underneath. It had only been an hour since we spoke on the phone so he hadn't had time to get the cars out. He also informed me that he contacted another collector who was coming over later that morning to look at the collection as well. I soon learned that the other collector was the guy with the classified ad just below mine that said that he buys all old toys.

Now my competitive juices started to flow, thinking that if I didn't leave with this collection, no matter what it looks like, I lose. I never liked to lose at anything, and this situation was no exception. He asked me to sit down at the small table in his kitchen while he went down into the basement to fetch the cars. I had no idea what was going to walk up those steps and certainly was not prepared for what happened over the next sixty minutes.

On his first trip up from the basement he brought a box full of Flying Color blister packs that looked like they were just bought at the local toy store. Flying Colors were a line-up of Hot Wheels that were introduced in 1974. I began the task of going through them and started to catalogue each car on my note pad as I always did, and began the process of appraising the collection. As my head was down and hyper-focused on the cars in front of me that totaled around 50, I was soon surrounded by four more boxes that seemed to magically appear from the basement. I looked around in amazement and asked the silly question, "Is this all you got?" He gazed at me, didn't make a peep as he stood up and headed back down the basement steps for what appeared to be one final trip. I was being a bit sarcastic, but my question must have jogged his memory. This time it wasn't a large box, but a small black vinyl case about ten inches long by two inches high.

To say that I was overwhelmed was truly an understatement. I was surrounded by five large boxes of what appeared to be all blister packs from 1968 to1977. For whatever reason that day, I emptied out my savings account and had all the cash to my name in my front pocket. Travelling into Philly with this much cash is not the smartest idea, but I just had a strange feeling that I would need it, and every penny of it.

Now I was in the zone, the incredible, once in a lifetime, original one owner amazing collection zone. I couldn't believe that this was happening to me. It was a collection that dreams were made of in the collecting world. The gentleman sat there quietly lighting up a cigarette every twenty minutes or so and watching me every step of the way. Not that he didn't trust me, I don't think he trusted anybody. So I carried on with the appraisal process for the next couple of hours and we made some small talk during that time. My first question was how he accumulated such an amazing collection. He began by telling me that his brother passed away suddenly in 1967, and left a four year old son behind. The gentleman went on to explain that he worked for the streets department in the City of Philadelphia, installing, repairing, and replacing signs along all the city streets and roadways. During his time on the road, he would pass a Kiddie City or Two Guys department store occasionally that were on his route. He said that he would stop in a few times a week in one or both of the stores and purchase every model of Hot Wheels over the next ten years. He went on to tell me the reason why he purchased Hot Wheels was for his nephew. He kind of took over the role of being his father and wanted him to enjoy his childhood as much as any other kid his age at the time.

Hot Wheels were his nephew's favorite toy so he wanted to make sure he had at least one of every model for him, but he would also buy a duplicate of each car in case he really liked a particular model and wanted another of the same. He explained that his nephew never asked for any of the duplicate cars he had purchased for him and was happy just playing with one car of each casting. The collection had one and sometimes two in the original blister pack as I discovered. The gentleman also told me that, if he personally really liked a car, he would buy a couple extras just so he could have one for himself as well. The collection was jaw dropping to say the least. After a couple of hours of cataloguing each and every blister pack, I moved onto the little black case not knowing what to expect. I was blown away with what I saw next.

I asked if I could look in the black case and he said, "Of course." I proceeded to slowly unsnap the button on the side and there they were, one of the most amazing grouping of eight Hot Wheels cars I had ever laid eyes on to this day. I fell back in my chair and asked him what the story was behind this little grouping of cars. He proceeded to pull an old letter out of his pocket. It was a letter from Mattel. He said that, back in the '60s and early '70s, he became frustrated because he couldn't find certain castings in any of the local toy stores. So he decided to write Mattel and voice his displeasure. He then showed me an old dusty note book that listed every car Mattel produced for each year starting in 1968 and ending in 1977. This guy really knew what he was doing back then.

The log he kept was so well organized that he truly did not miss a trick and not a single casting slipped by him. He told me that he wrote the letter listing the eight castings that weren't available in the Philadelphia region at the time for whatever reason, and dropped it in the mail. The response from Mattel took about eight weeks according to the gentleman, but they certainly came through in a big way, a real big way. I read the letter from Mattel and it was so professionally written and apologetic that I was totally impressed even more with the company. Along with the letter, they sent the eight castings he was missing, just not in the blister pack. All loose cars, but oh my goodness, I cannot even imagine what their values would have been if they were actually placed in the blister pack back then.

The contents of this little black case would impress any collector. The eight cars present in the little black vinyl case were as follows: 1. Watermelon Custom Mustang 2. Lite blue Custom Corvette 3. Orange Classic Cord 4. Purple Bye Focal 5. Yellow Superfine Turbine 6. Lime green Show Off 7. Magenta Short Order 8. Red Openfire

Not only was I blown away with all the blister packs, but now these eight little gems in mint condition were sitting right in front of me. I started to sweat a bit as I didn't want to lose this collection to the next guy scheduled to be there in only thirty minutes. I needed to move and move fast if I were to take this incredible collection home with me. If I didn't pull this off, no one, and I mean no one would have believed me as to what was in front of me. I proceeded to pull out my envelope of cash and laid it on the table. His eyes immediately locked on the envelope, and at that point, I knew I had the upper hand. He blurted out that he really needed the money for a new hot water heater. I took the money out of the envelope one note at a time, and showed him everything I had. I spread it across the table and he pondered my offer for about three minutes, but it felt like an eternity. He started to round up my cash and at that same moment he said, "Deal, I accept your offer." I was, for the first time in my life, speechless.

I was so excited to get the unbelievable collection home to share with my collector buddies, especially Todd and John. As soon as I packed up and got in my car, I got on the phone, and reached out to Todd first, then John. I always called them after I found a collection. I ripped through the little neighborhood of Tacony with the feeling of the tires on my car never touching the asphalt, and potholes of course. By the time I got back over the bridge and into Jersey to my home, waiting patiently there in their respective vehicles were, you guessed it, Todd and John. Todd looked at me as he always did when I scored a nice collection, and just laughed in his own infectious way. "What did you get this time?" he asked. I just smiled and asked him and John to help me carry the boxes in my house. I always would lay out each collection, no matter how big or small, on the dining room table, and this time was no different except that there was barely enough room for all the cars.

The collection ended up totaling 237 blister packs and eight loose cars. Everything was basically in mint condition due to how the cars were stored. The astonishing aspect of how this gentleman collected was in his choice of colors for each casting. He had great taste and seemed to acquire a lot of the rarest colors, including alternates, in all the cars he purchased right out of the store. He may have not known it at the time, but he was truly a genius and master collector in his own right.

Every single car in the collection had red line tires, every one of them. I've already covered the loose cars Mattel sent, so now let's move on to the blister packs, all 237 of them. The '68s were not complete as they were missing the Mustang and Corvette. The highlights from that year were a purple Custom Camaro, lite blue Eldorado, and creamy pink Custom VW. The '69 blisters didn't disappoint either. The highlights from that year were the magenta Classic '31 Ford Woody and rose VW Beach Bomb. The interesting side note about the rose VW Beach Bomb is that it was one of Todd's favorite castings in one of his favorite colors. I handed the car to Todd and said he could have it. It was my gift to a true collector friend who's company and conversation I still enjoy to this day. He was thrilled and couldn't thank me enough. He still has the car displayed proudly in his office. Let's move on to 1970. The highlights in the collection from that year were the hot pink Ambulance, purple Heavy Chevy, and purple Porsche 917. 1971 was proudly represented by the rose Boss Hoss, hot pink Cockney Cab, and purple Jet Threat. 1972 produced the aqua C-111 Mercedes and rose Side Kick.

The following year, 1973, was the year of the enamels. Mattel had to cut production costs due to the economy and the beautiful spectra-flame paints were now just a memory. The '73s in this collection were complete, with a few surprises like the lime green Ferrari 312P, dark blue

Mercedes-Benz C-111, red Mongoose, light blue Odd Job, lemon yellow Porsche 917, light blue Prowler, dark blue Street Snorter, yellow Snake, lime green Sweet Sixteen, and dark blue Xploder. The only thing missing from this year was the Shell Gas Station promos.

The years, 1974 through 1977 were complete for every casting as well, but the highlights in these years were truly not for the faint of heart. Alternate colors (usually limited production) in duplicate and triplicate were scattered throughout. Three green Heavy Chevys, two plum Odd Rods, two blue El Rey Specials, one light green Prowler, two red Porsche 917's, one dark blue Rash 1, two light green Sir Rodney Roadsters, one light green Chevy Monza 2+2, two white Mustang Stockers, two light green Vega Bombs, and two Show Hoss's. The extent and depth of this collection was truly impressive and unbelievable to most collectors, especially when they saw it with their own eyes.

I ended up selling off all the cars from 1974 through 1977 for a couple of reasons. First and foremost, I was out of money and needed to replenish my bank account. Secondly, my focus always was on the years that I collected as a child, 1968 through 1972. Todd was a master at selling cars on ebay and he got right to it over the next six months. He acted as my broker for many years, selling all the overflow from the collections I had purchased.

The Tacony collection was on a level I thought I would never see again in my collecting career, but I was wrong. But it would take another 14 years until the next collection of this magnitude would show its beautiful face to me.

Some of the original blister packs from the Tacony collection

CHAPTER NINE

The Recent Discoveries

I ended up selling off my entire collection in 2008 because I needed to finally pay off all my nine years of college loans. Sadly, even my childhood cars were included in the sale. I kept on collecting for a few more years after that, but the collections had pretty much dried up through the channels I was still using to dig them up. I ended up leaving the hobby for a few years to focus more on my growing business, Geese Chasers, LLC. Fast forwarding to the year 2016, I jumped back in, head first, to the hobby that I still missed and loved. I've had incredible success over the last couple of years with my new strategy of acquiring original one owner collections. I was now casting my net over the entire continental USA with all my efforts. I wanted to share some of my more interesting and mind-blowing collections I've uncovered since 2016.

The Windsor Colorado Collection

The collection arrived via the United States Postal Service in a medium sized box that was left on my doorstep on November 21, 2016. The total count of cars was 60. They came in a 48-car stack case along with a 24-car flat case. Each car had either its metal or plastic button proudly displayed next to it in their respective case. The back story to this collection was the gentleman had the cars since childhood and needed to unload them due to a job transfer that took him across the country. The cars, generally speaking, were very well kept and some were more played with than others. The collection produced a car that I'd been chasing for well over two decades at this point. One of my all time favorite castings is the Short Order, and as stated earlier, my favorite color is purple. A purple Short Order is ridiculously hard to find in any condition. This collection ended up having a blister pack fresh example of the car and I was blown away when I took it out of the case. Patience in this hobby is truly a virtue. In my many years of collecting and searching out original collections, the cars that you think will never show up, all eventually do.

The rest of the collection certainly didn't disappoint at any level. There was a mint lite green Evil Weevil, orange with white interior Light My Firebird, brown '36 Ford Coupe, and olive Cockney Cab. There were many other cars in near mint to mint condition as well, but mainly in somewhat common colors. Truly a great find out of Colorado.

The Windsor Colorado collection proudly on display

Purple Short Order and Lite Green Evil Weevil

The Carrier Mills Illinois Collection

During the time I received the collection from Colorado, I was already working on a new find out of Carrier Mills, Illinois. It ended up being a collection that no one in the family had any interest in, and the owner wanted it to go in the hands of a collector like myself. I graciously obliged the gentleman. I appraised the collection through the many pictures and videos of the cars that were sent to me, and I made an offer as I typically did on a collection of this quality. The gentleman was extremely pleased with my offer and couldn't believe the value of his childhood collection. The collection arrived in one large box, on my doorstep, on November 23, 2016.

I was very excited to see the cars in person, knowing that there were some very valuable and mint pieces from the pictures I reviewed. The total number of cars in the collection was 50 and they were from the years 1968 through 1975. Nine of the cars were from the hallowed year 1973 and they were all pretty much flawless, which is always a good thing, especially with the enamels such as these. The cars that really stood out to me as part of this collection due to their color, condition, and castings were as follows: Pink Sweet 16, red Dune Daddy, yellow Odd Job, yellow Prowler, and Police Cruiser. All pretty much mint and rare, very rare. The rest of the collection had some desirable pieces in good shape, but nothing compared to the '73s. A great find out of Illinois.

The Carrier Mills collection on display

The Collingswood New Jersey Collection

Growing up in the South Jersey area, it was ironic that I would score a collection all the way from my new home in San Diego California, but it happened, and my collector friends back east still haven't forgiven me. I got the call from an older gentleman that said he'd been a collector of the old Hot Wheels his entire life. He was too old to have grown up with them, but he still had a great appreciation for the cars from the Redline era, 1968 to 1977. This collection took a bit more time to negotiate than most. I was dealing with a fellow New Jerseyan after all, and we both understood each other quite well. He wanted to get full retail for his years of collecting, so I had advised him, like I always do, to investigate online auction sites like ebay. Ebay typically is the daily standard measure of value of what any collectible is being sold for at any given time. Hot Wheels are no exception, and most people that approach me when considering selling me their collections, typically start the conversation with, "I looked on ebay and this is what my cars are worth." Most individuals make the mistake of looking at the top listing in relation to the car they are investigating and only look at the BUY IT NOW price. This is how most people determine a car's value on ebay regardless of the color or condition of the piece. It is inaccurate to say the least, but try explaining that to most people.

We went back and forth for well over a month and I finally decided to call my friend Todd to see if he could meet with the gentleman and give him his opinion on value as well. Todd agreed and the meeting was set. Todd looked over the collection and shared his thoughts with the older gentleman. Todd then decided to facetime me from the man's smoke-filled basement where the collection was housed. After going through most of the collection, Todd and I both agreed on the collection's value. I spoke with the gentleman and told him to sit on my offer, which I felt was more than fair, and in the meantime explore his options on ebay. He agreed and we said our goodbyes.

Two weeks later to the day, my cell phone rang and on the other end of the phone was the owner of the collection. He said that he thought it over and considered all of his options, and came to the conclusion that my offer was fair. The deal was done and the cars were packed and on the way to the west coast.

The cars arrived in a large box on my front porch on March 10, 2017. The collection totaled 76 cars with three collector buttons and a mint-in-box Hot Wheels Dual Lane Rod Runner Hand Shift Power Booster. The cars arrived in three 24 count generic car cases. The gentleman collected only the first ten years of production, and there were some rare pieces scattered throughout. The cars that have the most value in this collection are the two Superfine Turbines in dark and lite blue, two Odd Jobs in pink and yellow, a yellow Prowler, a green Classic Cord, and a magenta Openfire. All cars are in near mint to mint condition and are all well sought after in the hobby to this day. The rest of the collection was almost equally as impressive with ten hot pinks, two purple VW Beach Bombs, an icy blue McClaren M6A, a rose pink Classic '31 Ford Woody, and a white interior red King Kuda. All in all it was a really good day, thanks to the Garden State.

The Collingswood collection on display

The Covington Indiana Collection

The mid-west has produced a lot of collections for me over the past 24 months. I got the call in March of 2017 from a man who wanted to sell his collection of Hot Wheels. It was a collection on the smaller end, but don't let size fool you. The cars contained were mainly in mint condition and almost half of them were customs. I went through all the usual bevy of questions and procedures in evaluating and appraising a collection from out-of-state. We agreed on a price and the deal was completed. The cars where packed and shipped the same day.

The collection arrived in a smaller box than usual due to the size of the overall collection. The total number of cars was 34 along with all of their respective collectors buttons. The most amazing and stand out piece in the collection was a blinding gold Custom Charger and nuclear shade of salmon pink Sand Crab. The other superstars were the shiny aqua black roof, white interior Custom Camaro, blazing lite blue Ford Mk IV, aqua McClaren M6A, red with white interior Custom Mustang, orange Custom Eldorado, and lime yellow Custom Corvette. All in all it was a tiny collection that packed a big punch in the end.

The Covington collection on display

Gold Custom Charger

The Pittsburgh Pennsylvania Collection

One of the more impressive collections over the past two years has been the Pittsburgh Pennsylvania collection. The overall condition of practically every car in the collection is basically mint. Hard to believe after all these years, but the pictures do not lie. This collection was also on the smaller size, but again, it's all about condition for me as a collector. The gentleman who reached out to me worked for a company that did home and estate clean outs. He told me that on a recent job, he came across the two cases of cars in an attic shoved way out of sight in the furthest corner away from everything. Apparently he almost left without them until his boss told him to make one final sweep confirming that everything was completely removed from the premises. It was only then that he came upon the two cases. I can understand how this collection was almost missed. The cars were kept in two Rally Cases, one 12-car and one 24-car case. Rally Cases are black and can get lost in the scenery of a typical, dark attic.

The cars in their respective cases arrived on June 19, 2017. I was even more impressed when I had the cars in front of me as to their overall condition. The cars that were at the top of the heap are as follows; Shiny gold with white interior Custom Mustang, olive Light My Firebird, hot pink Custom AMX, creamy pink with a white interior and black roof Custom T-Bird, brown with white interior Custom Eldorado, olive Custom Corvette, and a beautiful lite blue Lola GT70. Another stunning collection uncovered and now in my stable. A collection any passionate collector would cherish and be proud of.

The Pittsburgh collections arrival

The Pittsburgh collection on display

The Pittsburgh collection highlights

The Rockville Connecticut Collection

Over the past two years, the majority of my collections have been discovered mainly in the mid-west and northeast regions of this great country of ours. The Rockville, Connecticut collection also fell into one of these categories. This was another impressive collection based on condition and a few rare pieces. The collection was being sold by a gentleman who worked independently cleaning out people's homes that fell into foreclosure. He was typically hired by banks and lending institutions once the homes were vacated by the previous owners. He told me that the collection was found in a downstairs closet in a box with a lot of other miscellaneous items. The collection meant nothing to him except how much he could sell it for. He texted me four shots of each car, in focus the first time for a change, and I appraised the collection. Appraisals typically take me twenty four to forty hours to complete because of the extensive research that is required at times for some of the rarer pieces that a collection may hold. I made him an offer and he accepted it within a day.

The collection arrived in a medium sized box on November 1, 2017. The cars were placed in three identical 24-car cases. The years of production for the cars ranged from 1968 to 1972. A total of six customs, including a glowing, hot pink with white interior Custom Eldorado which was the star of this show. Other notable pieces were the creamy pink Hot Heap and orange '36 Ford Coupe, both minty. The rest of the cars were either commons or mid-range cars, but their overall condition is what made this collection stand out to the crowd.

The Rockville Connecticut collection

The Rockville Connecticut collection on display

The Rockville Connecticut collection highlights

The Las Vegas Nevada Collection

Every once in a while I hit upon a group of cars that totally shocks even me after all these years, while at the same time producing a car that I never thought in a million years would show up in an original one owner childhood collection. The Las Vegas collection is one of these rare instances where I even had to take a seat after what I discovered hiding out amongst all the other cars. It was late in the year 2017, and we were only one week away from Christmas, my favorite time of year. My cell phone rang, and on the other end of the line was a gentleman who had just emptied out his storage unit and was looking to unload his childhood collection of Hot Wheels. A job transfer motivated him to sell off a lot of his personal items He was another individual who wanted the collection to be taken care of as well as he had as a child. We discussed my philosophy on preserving the history of the collections and keeping the collection intact and it was music to his ears. He facetimed with me and we went over the entire group of sixty seven Redline Hot Wheels and two Fat Daddy Sizzlers. Fat Daddy Sizzlers are a very rare find, and I was happy to see them pop up in this outstanding collection. The collection also included a 24-car Rally Case and 48-car flat case, but the biggest surprise wouldn't be revealed until after I received the cars. I appraised the cars and had the information and my offer to him within 24 hours. He was more than happy with my offer and accepted immediately. The cars were shipped out priority the next day.

The collection arrived in a large flat box because of the shape of the 48 and 24-car cases that contained all the cars. I was excited to finally see the cars in person because they certainly left a lasting impression on me during facetime. Once again, I was pleasantly surprised by the overall condition of the cars. They looked even better in person than over the internet. It was a very impressive collection even before I made the astonishing discovery that still had eluded me. There was a rainbow of all the best colors in the collection, and this truly made it special in my world. The colors represented in multiple castings were lite blue, antifreeze, orange, aqua, purple, and hot pink. An assortment of customs, spoilers, and grand prix cars rounded out the bunch. The collection encompassed cars produced from the years 1968-1973 , skipping the year 1972 completely.

What happened next is a story that I will never forget. Over the years, after receiving a collection and putting it out on display, I always would go through and study each car in case I missed something or could possibly learn something new. In the case of this collection, it was the common casting of the Peeping Bomb that shook my world momentarily. The Peeping Bomb was originally introduced in 1970 and released with Mattel's new line up that year. There were two colors, purple and orange (my two favorite colors of course) that were released early in production with orange painted headlights and were once thought to be prototypes. Today they are considered early production runs and are extremely rare and very difficult to find, especially in a collection like this. Well, this collection included a mint orange Peeping Bomb. The Peeping Bomb has a plastic black lever that exposes the silver headlights when pulled back. The lever pushed forward closes the headlights. While finishing up my review of the collection in hand, I finally got around to the Peeping Bomb. Like I've done hundreds and hundreds of times before, I pulled back on the lever to see the color of the headlights. Up to this point, the headlights were always, and I means always, silver. To my astonishment and disbelief, the headlights were ORANGE. I just couldn't believe, that after all these years, I finally hit an orange headlight Peeping Bomb. Christmas had arrived early in the Young household. It was truly a great moment for me as a collector and one I will not soon forget.

The Las Vegas collection upon arrival

The orange headlight Peeping Bomb

The Ione California Collection

Even though Hot Wheels birthplace is the beautiful state of California, I rarely hit any collections from there. Ione, California had a hidden gem of a collection that wasn't discovered by me until most recently. The collection was owned by an individual who was looking to make some money on something that was just collecting dust at his house. Most of the cars were in excellent condition with a handful of what we call "beaters" in the hobby. These cars have signs of having been well played with, like chipped paint or worn wheels. Pretty typical compared to most of the collections I've bought over my career.

The appraisal was finished through the review of hundreds of photos that were emailed to me and my offer was submitted. The individual accepted my offer after shopping around the collection for a week, and the deal was completed. The cars arrived January 22, 2018. A total of 57 loose cars and one blister pack completed the lot, along with three 12-car Rally Cases. The uniqueness of the collection for me was the fact that it was a near perfect representation of the collections that most of us children of the '60s enjoyed and actually owned. The highlights were a hot pink Custom Charger, purple Sugar Caddy, Aqua and lite green Porsche 917, and near perfect Police Cruiser. All are some of my favorite castings as a child and now. Finally a really cool collection from my new home state of California and it felt good.

The IONE collection just opened

The IONE CA collection

In Memory of…..

The Wichita Kansas Collection

Every once in a while I'll hit a collection with a story that brings tears to my eyes, and the Wichita Kansas collection is just one of them. I received a phone call after the holidays from a nice gentleman out of state who still had his childhood collection of Hot Wheels and wanted them to end up in the hands of a collector that would proudly care for them and display them. I never make any promises to display a collection, because I literally would need an extra house next door if I were to do so. Only the most interesting and significant collections are placed on my wall of fame in my office for all to see. As time went on during our conversation, the gentleman told me that his intention was always to leave the collection to his son. Tragically, his son was killed in an automobile accident recently and there was no one else to leave the collection to in his family.

I told him how truly sorry I was for his loss and said a prayer for him and his family. We moved into the appraisal process and agreed on a price when all was said and done. His final question to me was if his collection had made it to my wall of fame. I said a resounding yes, and told him that I would be proud to place his collection amongst some of my greatest discoveries. He was thrilled and had one final request for me, and that was to dedicate the collection to his son that he most recently lost. I didn't hesitate for a second and agreed.

The collection arrived on January 23, 2018, and totaled fifty-six Redline Hot Wheels, and one gold Johnny Lightning called the Mad Maverick. The collection spanned the years 1968-1976. Also included in the collection was a Stunt Action Set in box, Hot Strip Track Pak in box, lots of collector buttons, multiple sticker sheets, a 48-car, flat carrying case, two Sizzlers, a Juice Machine, lots of Sizzlers accessories, a 1970 International Collectors Catalog, and the coveted Hot Wheels Club Magazine. All kept together just as they arrived, now lit up on display *In Memory of Andrew Truesdell*. May God rest his soul.

The Wichita KS collection complete

The Wichita KS collection proudly on display

In memory of....

The Blacksburg Virginia Collection

The date was March 7, 2018. I was on a business trip back east in New Jersey when my phone rang. On the phone was a gentleman who had a collection of old Hot Wheels that were from the Blacksburg, Virginia area. I asked him how he acquired them and he went on to tell me that the gentleman whom he had purchased the cars from, bought them from a friend who owned a general store back in the '60s and '70s. He further elaborated that when the store closed, the gentleman had purchased all the cars that were either left on the pegs or in the back stockroom. Needless to say, the entire collection of 106 cars were all in their original blister packs. Part of the collection was also purchased from an old gas station that also closed its doors. They would give them away with a purchase of 10 dollars or more of gasoline. The reason for this part of the collection with the cards cut in half was due to the metal collector's buttons that were deemed too dangerous for children due to its sharp tab at the top that could potentially cause an injury.

The collection was massive in total number, especially due to the fact that they all were still in their original packaging. We eventually met at a mutually agreed upon location, and when the box was opened, it almost knocked me to the ground. The amount of blister packs was quite overwhelming considering they were found in one place and part of the same collection. Hard to believe that this was less than half of the largest blister pack collection I ever purchased, but that was a long time ago, and collections like this, obviously only come around every 20 years.

The highlights of the collection were as follows; Three Rose Pink Beach Bombs, twenty-two Spoilers including an aqua Evil Weevil and a purple Light My Firebird, twenty-four Grand Prix's, three Custom Corvettes, three Custom VW's, two Custom Chargers, and three Custom AMX. The rest of the cars were rounded out with some mid-range cars and commons. It was a good day to be a collector for sure.

The entire Blacksburg VA collection

Some of the highlights from the Blacksburg VA collection

The Susanville California Collection

The call came in from a young man that I surmised to be in his late twenties to early thirties. He politely asked if he had reached the right guy to sell his grandfather's Hot Wheels collection. I, of course, said that he had come to the right place and asked how could I help him. He had taken pictures of the collection and immediately texted them to me on my cell phone. The cars looked as if they had just came off the production line at Mattel. I asked the young man if he knew the story behind how his grandfather came across the cars. He said that his grandmother told him that, back in the late '60s and early '70s, her husband would stop by the local convenience stores and buy a car if it caught his eye. She went on to tell her grandson that he never took any out of the packages, but he enjoyed looking at them just as well.

The cars were put away in 1971 and only taken out periodically over the years for a quick glance or two. Fortunately the cars spent their entire lives in a dry warm climate in California, and showed very little if any of the effects of temperature change and humidity in regards to the paint, cardboard, and plastic. The collection numbered 26 cars in total and they were all as nice as I've seen over my career.

All the cars were all-stars in my book, but the Most Valuable Players were as follows; orange with black roof and white interior King Kuda (considered by collectors to be the Holy Grail of this casting), green with white interior Carabo, blue with white interior Heavy Chevy, two light green Sugar Caddy's, two magenta Sea Siders, an aqua Boss Hoss, and a blue Volkswagen Beach Bomb. The remainder of the collection were mid-range and a few commons. It was another stellar find and, this time, thankfully from a climate that truly helped preserve their beauty.

The entire Susanville blister pack collection

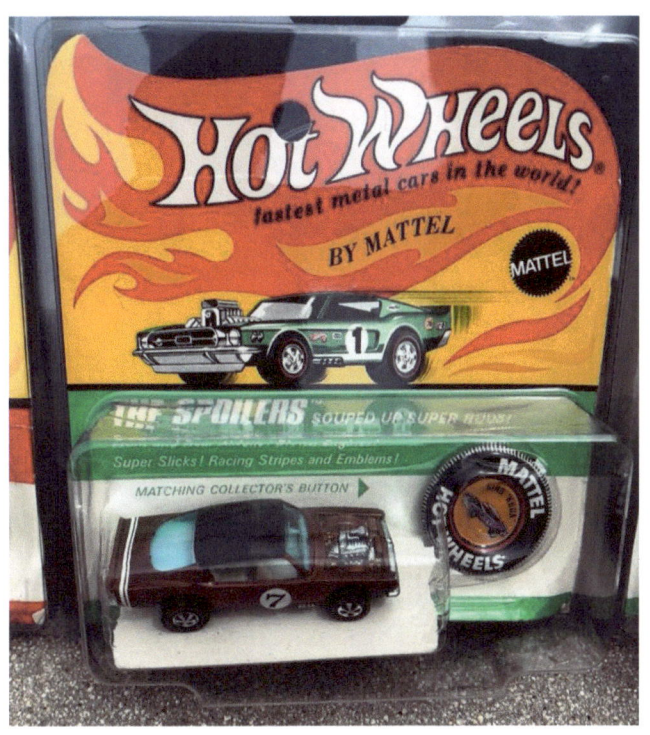

The Holy Grail of the King Kuda casting

Green with white interior Carabo blister pack

The Crème de la Crème

Part Deaux

The Tucson Arizona Collection

Well, it only took another 14 years, but it happened for a second time in my collecting career. I again uncovered a once-in-a-lifetime original one-owner childhood collection that truly rivals the huge blister pack collection I discovered almost a decade and a half earlier in Tacony, Pennsylvania. Oddly, the names of both towns started with the letter "T" and had six total letters. Just an interesting side note to these two incredible finds.

The call came in at exactly 2:57 PM on Tuesday May 2, 2017. This time I was sure to retrace my steps and document every last detail once I realized the magnitude of the collection that was now within my grasp. The gentleman on the other end of the line was a very nice, friendly, and jovial soul. Our initial conversation went extremely well. He told me a lot about his life and exactly how he came upon the collection, and boy what a collection it was.

He was a retired postman of thirty plus years, living in Tucson, Arizona with his beloved wife. He went on to talk about his children and grandchildren that lived in southern California, not too far from me. As the conversation approached the 10 minute mark, it shifted, and then the collection was the main topic at hand. The gentleman told me that he had initially shopped the collection locally. He also drove to Phoenix to meet another Hot Wheels collector who only offered him 1000 dollars. He had not accepted the offer because he felt the collection could possibly be worth quite a bit more. Let's back up a bit to how and when he came across this gem of a collection.

The collection was discovered at a little yard sale on the outskirts of Tucson, Arizona on Saturday April 22, 2017. The gentleman and his wife loved to hit yard sales on the weekend. They would religiously plan out their Saturdays and Sundays well in advance, based on the local yard sales close to home. The collection was sitting on a woman's front lawn and consisted of five large original Hot Wheels stack cases loaded with cars. There was also a five-gallon painter's bucket that went along with the collection that was overflowing with car parts, wheels, interiors, axles, etc.. The gentleman inquired about the collection, and the woman told him that her husband had recently passed and they were his cars. This was all the detail relayed to me regarding any type of background on the collection. The woman was asking 10 dollars a case, 10 DOLLARS A CASE! The gentleman just had a feeling that the cars were worth something but realized that he only had 40 dollars in his wallet. He asked the woman if she would take 8 dollars a case and she quickly accepted his offer. After completing the morning of yard sales, he and his wife headed home with the cars.

The couple considered giving the five cases of cars to some of their grandkids to play with, but thought that they should look into their values first. He stated that he knew they had to have some value solely due to their age. The few collectors that had looked the cars over had only offered him 1000 dollars or less for the entire lot. According to him, that was what motivated him to search out a reputable collector on the internet. That's when he came across the Redline Archeology website and contacted me. I discussed my philosophy of collecting the old Hot Wheels and showed him some pictures of the many collections already on display in my office. He seemed to really enjoy the information and seeing the collections on display. By now, we had developed a level of trust and mutual respect which allowed us to move into the next phase, the appraisal.

I further discussed with him how the whole process works with sending me pictures, in focus and from four different angles, for a proper and accurate estimate of values. He was agreeable to all steps along the way and got right to sending me all the individual pictures of all the cars in the entire collection. I was totally floored as each new picture popped up on my phone. Every picture demonstrated yet another mint car and it was consistent through much of the collection. I had my work cut out for me as I had to basically go through over 1000 pictures and evaluate almost 300 of the most beautiful and rare Redlines I've ever seen assembled in one collection. It was truly a collection that raised a lot of questions in my mind. Sometimes cars are so rare that the original owner was actually a salesman or Mattel employee.

The appraisal was completed in three days, working until midnight each day, in addition to running my business. It was a huge undertaking, but one I enjoyed every step of the way. I was still in disbelief, and actually wondered if I was being pranked or the butt of someone's joke. I called the gentleman and discussed the collection piece by piece like I always do, spending the most time on the rarest and cleanest pieces. I have to give the guy credit, he listened intently for at least two hours straight before asking any questions. I could sense that his wife was listening in on the call as well, and they both had huge smiles on each of their faces. After about a two and a half hour conversation about all the specifics and details surrounding the collection, it was time for me to make him an offer.

I was nervous yet very confident with the number I was offering but felt it was more than fair, and was hopeful that he would accept. The gauntlet was laid down and those words were spoken that always made me doubt myself, "I'll have to think about it and get back to you." The wind was immediately taken from my sails. It was a reality that I had to accept and live with. Over the next two days, I waited patiently for the phone to ring, and it did. The gentleman called me back and said these exact words, "I discussed your offer with the boss (his wife), and if you're willing to pay us that kind of money, we're willing to drive the cars to you." He said that it was the perfect excuse to visit his children and grandchildren who lived in the next town over from me. We decided to meet at a local coffee shop the following Monday, May 15. This was the earliest they could get out to California to meet me and see their kids and grandkids. It felt like an eternity waiting for that day to arrive, but it finally did, and the rest is Redline history.

I pulled up to the coffee shop, and could see the couple from the parking lot 100 feet away. They were sitting at a table outside with five cases of original Hot Wheels. When you've been doing this for as long as I have, you can spot the cars, cases, and accessories from a mile away.

It's hard to explain but it just gets in your blood and your soul. I walked up and introduced myself, and offered each of them a drink or bite to eat. I calmly and coolly excused myself and went inside to get my medium sized chai tea skim latte. Come on, give me a break, I'm trying not to leave out any part of this incredible story. Ok, let's get back to the story.

I got my drink and headed back outside. Thankfully they were both still there and didn't ditch me, which was certainly running through my mind. The collection still wasn't mine and I was a bit paranoid until the money and cars changed hands. I explained to the nice couple that I needed to verify that the cars were original and that there weren't any reproductions or repaints and they understood. I started going through each case, tray by tray, and car by car. They were all legit and all in mint un-played with condition for the most part. My body was starting to go into a minor state of shock at this time, so I needed to get the deal done before I passed out and ended up in the back of an ambulance. I sat down in front of both of them and started to count out the money, an amount many times greater than their other offer. They were extremely happy with the deal and were over the moon to say the least. As always when doing a deal in person, I have the individual or individuals count out the money agreed on right in front of me before I leave with the collection, just so there are no issues afterwards.

The money was accounted for and confirmed, so we shook on the deal. I packed up all five cases and started walking to my car when I heard the gentleman yell to me, "Hey, do you want these two little baggies that came with the cars?." I said, "Sure," as I was flashing back to the Northeast Philly collection 15 years prior when the gentleman offered me two large trash bags full of goodies on my way out. As he was handing them to me, he went on to say that, "I was only going to throw them away, but thought I'd ask you first." The two little sandwich baggies looked innocent enough, so I just tossed them on the passenger seat in my car. The cases of cars were placed on the back seat, safe and sound.

I couldn't wait to get home and spend some time with the cars. It was truly one of, if not the single greatest find in my collecting career. To this day, I'm not convinced that this wasn't a former Mattel employee's collection. The cars I'm about to describe leave that question wide open to ponder. The two little baggies will soon tell a piece of the story that we may never know the entirety of it all. I cleared the large counter top in our kitchen and started to take the car trays out of each case one by one, and laid them all next to each other. All in all, there ended up being a total of 287 cars. There were some Revvers, Fat Daddy Sizzlers, and Rumblers in there as well, but the majority of the collection was mint loose Redline Hot Wheels from 1968. The details of the collection, to this day, have stunned many a long time collector. Those that have laid eyes on the collection just shake their heads in disbelief that something like this was still out there just waiting to be uncovered and brought out to the light of day. To think that this entire collection was sold at a local yard sale is truly unbelievable. You may want to sit down for the next part, as I will be describing the amazing cars that were part of this phenomenal original collection, and what was in those little baggies that almost found their way to the trash can. Fasten your seatbelt and get ready for take-off. Oh yeah, make sure your seat is in the upright position.

Let me start by saying that the contents of this collection still make me shake my head every time I pass by them in my office. I have them proudly displayed and lit up for the whole world to see. It truly is a sight for sore eyes, especially if you are a collector or one who grew up with this amazing toy from the '60s. I think the best approach to describing the cars found in this collection is to start in 1968. I will not bore you with every single car in the collection. I will only highlight the best of the best in my eyes, but keep in mind that virtually every car in this collection was barely touched and certainly never run down a track. So let's get started on this amazing journey.

Let me start this off by saying that you may be as shocked as I was the first time I heard about this collection, but it's only a natural reaction for any passionate collector like myself. The original 16 from 1968 are amongst the most coveted in the hobby. Here they are ladies and gentleman, the best of the best cars from the Tucson, Arizona Collection. Enjoy!

1968

Custom Barracudas – Six in total: Two GOLD with white interiors, two AQUA with white interiors, one PURPLE with white interior, and one BLUE with dark interior.

Custom Camaro – Three in total: One RED with black roof, one BLUE with black roof, and one LIME YELLOW with black roof.

Custom Corvette – Three in total: One RED with white interior, one LIME YELLOW with dark interior, and one BLUE with dark interior.

Custom Cougar – Five in total: One LIME YELLOW with dark interior and painted tooth, one ORANGE with dark interior, one ANTIFREEZE with no interior, one OLIVE with dark interior, and one BLUE with light blue interior.

Custom Fleetside – Four in total: Two PURPLE, one ORANGE, and one GREEN.

Custom Mustang – Five in total: One GOLD open hood scoop, one RED open hood scoop, one RED with dark interior, one BLUE with white interior, and one BLUE with dark interior.

Custom T-Bird – Six in total: One PURPLE with black roof and dark interior, two AQUA with black roof and white interiors, one GOLD with black roof and white interior, and two AQUA with black roof and dark interiors.

Custom Volkswagen – Five in total: One ANTIFREEZE with white interior, one PURPLE with dark interior, Two BLUE with dark interiors, and one GREEN with dark interior.

Deora – Three in total: one ANTIFREEZE, two PURPLE.

Hot Heap – Five in total: Two ANTIFREEZE, one GOLD with white interior, one ORANGE, and one BLUE with white interior.

1969

Custom Charger – Four in total: One HOT PINK, one GREEN, and two BLUE.

Twin Mill – Three in total: One ANTIFREEZE, and two PURPLE.

1970

Sky Show Fleetside – Four in total: Two HOT PINK, one light PURPLE, and one AQUA.

Carabo – Seven in total: One GREEN, one BLUE, one Magenta, two ROSE, and two YELLOW.

Classic Nomad – Eight in total: Three PURPLE, one YELLOW, two ROSE, one LIME YELLOW, and one BLUE.

Mod Quad – Four in total: One PURPLE, one YELLOW, one BLUE, and one RED.

Mongoose – Two in total: RED.

Porsche 917 – Six in total: One GREEN, one ROSE, one MAGENTA, two LIME YELLOW, and one GRAY ENAMEL.

Power Pad – Four in total: One BLUE, two HOT PINK, and one ROSE

Snake – Two in total: YELLOW.

1971

AMX/2 – Four in total: One PURPLE, one MAGENTA, one ROSE, and one GREEN.

Bugeye – Two in total: one HOT PINK and one GREEN.

Classic Cord – Eight in total: One HOT PINK, one LIME YELLOW, one PURPLE, two GREEN, two BLUE, and one MAGENTA.

Cockney Cab – Three in total: One ROSE, one YELLOW, and one GREEN.

Grass Hopper – Nine in total: One HOT PINK, one SALMON PINK, one GREEN, two ROSE, one MAGENTA, one RED, and two LIGHT GREEN.

Hairy Hauler – Seven in total: One PURPLE, one SALMON PINK, one BLUE, two MAGENTA, and two YELLOW.

The HOOD – Five in total: One ROSE, two MAGENTA, one GREEN, and one BLUE.

Nitty Gritty Kitty – One in total: BROWN

Olds 442 – Four in total: One LIGHT GREEN, one RED, one BLUE, and one MAGENTA.

1972

Mercedes C-111 – One in total: GOLD

1973

Here they are in no particular order:

Dark Blue BUZZ OFF

Red FERRARI 312P

Red MONGOOSE

White POLICE CRUISER

Lemon Yellow SHOW OFF

Yellow SNAKE

Lime Green BUGEYE

Lime Green PEEPING BOMB

Red STRIP TEASER

Lemon Yellow SWINGIN' WING

Dark Blue TWIN MILL

1974

Rodger Dodger – Two in total: PLUM

Mercedes-Benz C-111 – Two in total: One RED, one RED with the C-111 TAMPO (early production car)

As you can see, it was quite the collection. Some very interesting pieces that really make me scratch my head at times. There were (2) 72-car stack cases along with (3) 48-car stack cases. There were also the two little, plastic, zip lock baggies that were included, and what I was about to discover was certainly a first for me in this hobby.

I finally completed my preliminary review of the entire collection and I was somewhat mentally and physically drained. Trust me, you would have felt the same way with this collection in front of you. I kept thinking that this collection could have certainly been owned by a former Mattel employee from the vast array of un-played with cars contained within. What happened next certainly supported my theory.

The two, little plastic baggies, full of what appeared to be junk and trash, were now sitting right in front of me just screaming to be opened. I grabbed the first one and opened it. There were Hot Heap interiors, cut axles with one hub and wheel still hanging on for dear life, all types of different glass interiors, loose engines, surfboards, and lots of Redline wheels in all shapes and sizes. It was basically a Hot Wheels part's store all in one place.

I was now onto the final leg of this amazing journey, and little did I know that the best was yet to come. I grabbed the second baggie, and it appeared, at first glance, to be very similar to the first baggie that I had just gone through. The only difference was that it was more densely stuffed and there appeared to be some paper in it. I emptied out the baggie right next to the collection and all the cars that were spread out on the kitchen island. I started to see that there were some of the same things like motors, interiors, and lots of loose wheels and axles. Then it happened, like a train barreling down the tracks with no brakes. It hit me right in the face. The stickers. Hundreds of sticker sheets from the first four years of production. One hundred fifty-two Spoiler sheets, 25 Porsche 917 sheets, 31 Ferrari 312P sheets, and 97 flower sheets that came with the Classic Nomad or Volkswagen Beach Bomb. I know what you're probably thinking, what's the big deal with all these sticker sheets. The big deal is what came next.

While sorting out the over two hundred sticker sheets already mentioned, there were another 22 mint sticker sheets that showed their beautiful large stars. You guessed it, 22 of the most beautiful Olds 442 sticker sheets I've ever laid eyes on in my two and a half decades of collecting. I was literally knocked off my chair at the sight of these extremely rare sticker sheets. The amazing thing is that they were all found in one collection, and in a plastic baggie that almost ended up in a landfill somewhere in southern California. Just when you think that you've seen it all in the world of collecting, something as innocent as this happens. I was just glad it happened to me.

The amazing Tucson AZ collection

Some of the contents in the plastic baggie

Mercedes Benz C-111 early production with tampo

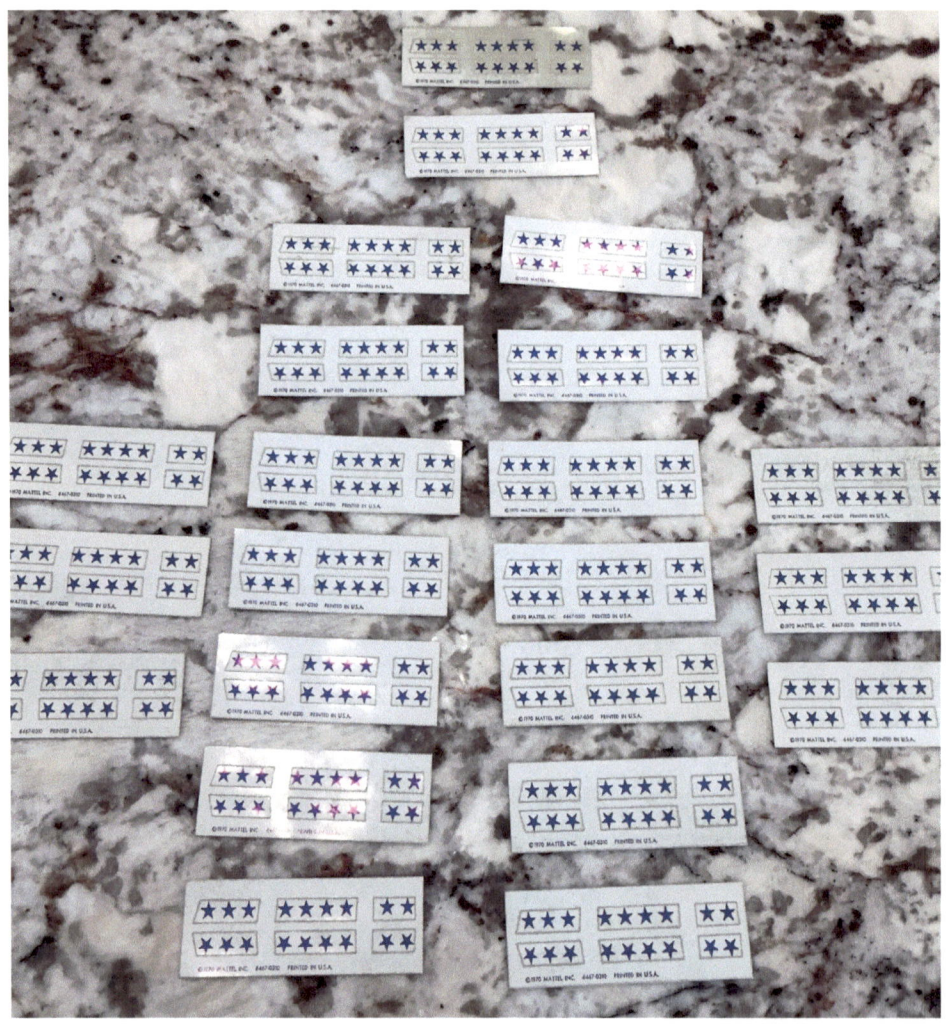

The OLDS 442 large star sticker sheets found in the Tucson AZ collection

The amazing Tucson AZ collection

The amazing Tucson AZ collection

Some highlights from the Tucson AZ collection

CHAPTER TEN

My Secrets Revealed

Over the last 25 years, the one question that I get directed at me by fellow collectors is, "How do you do it?" Early on it wasn't a secret, but everyone still had the impression that either I had a special formula or that I was just lucky. Well, I didn't have a secret formula that got me off the ground. It was just a simple, two-line classified ad that everyone eventually found out about. Oddly, it seemed that very few collectors were willing to spend the 100 bucks a week to run a classified ad to possibly acquire collections. For whatever reason, it never happened, and thus, I had no real competition. There was just the one guy in the paper that ran the "I buy old toys" ad next to mine. His ad was too general in my opinion, and mine was targeted for Hot Wheels and only Hot Wheels from the '60s and '70s. The other advantage I had was that my ad was above his, and that certainly gave me an edge. I'm sure he steered some collections away from me over the years, but I'm still convinced to this day, that I got the lion's share back then.

The arrival of ebay however, didn't deter my efforts as I continued to run the ad, but I did have to increase my marketing efforts and cast a bigger net. This was accomplished through pounding the pavement even more than before, placing my flyer on the bulletin boards of every small, medium, and large business that would allow me. I was now driving around to even more developments and businesses all over South Jersey, Delaware, Philadelphia and its suburbs. I was passing my business cards out at every opportunity that presented itself. As the fire died down with each passing year, I always kept the faith and never lost sight of what I was hoping to accomplish. I did score collections from time to time, but not nearly at the rate I did in the '90s, especially before ebay.

Let's recap. My first collection was purchased in September, 1993. It was discovered through a simple classified ad in the local Courier Post newspaper. I ran the same ad for the next eleven years, exclusively in the Philadelphia Inquirer, typically for the entire month of May, sometimes June, and occasionally in the fall. The first five years of running the classified ad were certainly the best years, as compared to the second five years. The reason for this, in my opinion, was the arrival of Auction Web in 1995, which eventually became ebay by 1997. Ebay was a game changer for me as the collections started to fall off a bit as we approached the year 2000. This was also around the time that I started my next crazy business venture, Geese Chasers, LLC. I was finishing up my third college degree, this time in Physician Assistant Studies at Hahnemann University in Philadelphia, PA, and came up with the idea that people would actually pay me to chase Canadian geese off their properties with my border collie named Boomer. Well, twenty years later, Geese Chasers, LLC is thriving and has franchise locations in five states. I reflect back on my childhood business of breeding tropical fish in 1972, and realized that my business philosophy and methods back then really weren't very different than now. I was truly a natural, and born to be in business. As the saying goes, "There are many men in business, but very few business men."

My wife Deborah, God bless her, has been so supportive of me and all my crazy ideas and dreams over the years. Her resiliency is unparalleled. She has never wavered once, and I truly love, appreciate, and respect her more than anyone I know. I can't imagine the type of roller coaster ride it must be for her or anyone that lives with an entrepreneur, frustrated archeologist, athletic trainer, and physician assistant all wrapped up in one. The real combination that continues to fuel my fire is the passionate archeologist that lives within me and the innate drive to be successful, while not having to answer to anyone, especially a boss.

Our third child Natalie was born in 2004 on Father's Day, and she was truly a blessing. My free time became more limited during this amazing stage of my life. My oldest daughter Madison was entering high school and our son Kyle was a travel ice and roller hockey player. My wife would take Madison to all her cheerleading practices and competitions, and I was Kyle's coach on his travel roller hockey team. At that point, my wife and I were truly outnumbered by our kids, and we went into a zone defense. Natalie went along for the ride to every hockey rink, cheerleading competition, and event. We quickly discovered that Natalie was a born gymnast, and by the age of two was flipping around the house, the bed, the trampoline out back, and everywhere else she could find. Now we had another athlete on our hands, and trips to the local gym were also part of our weekly schedule. As you can see, I had to shift gears and focus more on the family during this time, but I still made some time for the Hot Wheels.

It had been a year since scoring my last collection in 2008. I was still very involved with my kids' activities, and my business was growing rapidly, so I ended up taking a break from the hobby a couple years later in 2011. I put it out in the hobby world that I had decided to sell off my entire collection. Individuals were flying in from all over the country to see the collection first hand and make me an offer. This went on for about three months with many trips to the airport picking up fellow collectors and driving them to my home. I eventually sold off my entire collection to a couple of local collectors. It was a hard thing to do, but I needed the money at the time, and also needed to free up some more time for myself and family. I never stopped thinking about the cars and how many collections I missed out on from leaving the hobby for this brief period.

Things had calmed down as the kids were getting older, and my desire to get back in the game was stronger than ever in the spring of 2015. I really missed the cars, and especially the thrill I experienced with every collection discovery. I wanted to get back into the hobby and fast. We had recently moved out of New Jersey to the beautiful State of California the year prior for a change of scenery and to be near some friends and family. I was now tasked with how in the world was I going to approach finding original one owner Hot Wheels collections. Things had changed drastically since the days of classified ads, flyers, and business cards. The grass roots approach of going door to door was always a good thing, but canvassing neighborhoods is not allowed anymore. No more soliciting of any kind is permitted in most neighborhoods these days. I needed to come up with a strategy that made sense to me, but also packed the biggest punch.

I started reflecting back on the things that made my Geese Chasers, LLC business so successful over the years, and that's when it hit me. I needed to attack this through the internet. The first thing I did was contact my friend Larry who created and has managed my company website for over fifteen years. Larry and I discussed my latest idea and all he could do in the first five minutes was laugh and shake his head at me. I told him my whole back story and history of collecting, and how I needed to change up my approach, because the newspapers were, well, pretty much extinct.

The next thing Larry and I discussed was competition. The real question was if there was truly any real competition that existed in the hobby that we needed to address. Don't get me wrong, competition is a good thing, just not too much of it. Larry scoured the internet looking for competitors, and in his opinion, said it was pretty much a blank canvas, and we should do quite well with the right website and marketing approach. This was the green light I was waiting for. I had done my research as well and agreed with Larry. Collections were just waiting to be discovered, and who better than me I thought.

We sat down for hours and came up with a template that conveyed, what we thought, was the message we wanted to get across to the general public. The message I was trying to get across on the website was that of a long time collector, reputable, and willing to pay top dollar for the original Hot Wheels from the '60s and '70s. It wasn't a complicated formula, but one that had to be put together in a way that was understandable to the general public. Larry acquired pictures from me and other sources and started to build out a website from a template I had chosen weeks before. Start to finish, it took a solid six months while working out all the kinks. In the meantime, I started to try and build some excitement around the new website that was under construction. On March 13, 2016, I accomplished this by creating a Facebook page dedicated solely to Hot Wheels, which I named Redline Archeology. I actually ended up scoring a collection almost immediately because one of my former college lacrosse teammates saw it on my feed. The website was coming along nicely and I was getting anxious to see it go live. Some last minute changes were made towards the end that held things up a bit, but this is just how I roll at times. I wanted it to look and feel amazing, while at the same time hitting the mark.

The day had arrived, and it was time to launch the website for the whole world to see. The date was June 12, 2016. The day REDLINE ARCHEOLOGY dot com was born. Now all I needed to go along with the site was a marketing strategy. I've been told that a new website can take years to work its way up the food chain in regards to searches, especially one as niche as this. I decided to apply the same principles I have used successfully over the years with my company, Geese Chasers, LLC. I started a national Google ad word campaign for REDLINE ARCHEOLOGY dot com that covered the entire continental United States. My daily budget for the campaign was set, and we were off to the races. From how I understand it, it still takes some time to get traction in search engines even after starting a campaign like this. I waited patiently to see if my newly devised plan would work.

It wasn't until August when I finally started to reap the rewards from my investment. Thanks to the Google ad word campaign, I was able to gain the top spot in many of the search engines within two months. It did cost me though, but it was worth every penny. Collections started to roll in and they haven't stopped to this day.

The formula for my success nowadays is to first understand that you truly have a passion for this wonderful hobby of collecting Hot Wheels. Secondly, the only successful way that I know of acquiring collections today is to be diligent in your efforts. You must post on your social media outlets weekly, whether it's telling people you buy the old Hot Wheels or just post a fun fact and/or a collection you may have recently scored. True collectors enjoy learning more about the hobby they love, and also want to share in others' joy when a collection is discovered. In addition, collectors are really curious and interested to see what you have uncovered and brought to light. They also try to buy lots of cars off of you almost immediately, but that's understood. You must also update your website to keep it fresh with new pictures, videos, and stories about the collections you have acquired most recently. I recommend semi-annual website updates. Finally, make sure that you can afford to pay for a Google ad word campaign or something equally as relevant and effective. You cannot be undercapitalized when taking on a venture like this. You must spend money year round if you ever expect to score an original collection.

Some of my collection on display

More of my collection on display in my office

More of the Bob Young Collection

The most important thing, when you do come across an amazing find like an original Hot Wheels collection from the '60s or '70s, is to always be upfront and honest with the owner(s). Always offer a free no obligation appraisal of the cars first and foremost. If you cannot appraise the collection in person, be sure to get high definition pictures of each car from the front, back, both sides, top and bottom. Texting is a great way to receive pictures and nowadays seems to be the easiest method for the owner(s). Be sure to take your time and do the appraisal correctly by researching each car and accessory online, and then place what you think is the full retail value on the piece. Do this with each and every car and accessory you evaluate. It takes time, but if you are truly passionate about the hobby, you will enjoy every minute of it as I do. Once the appraisal is complete, speak to the owner and discuss the most valuable pieces first, and then work your way down. They will really appreciate your honesty and knowledge. This approach will certainly work to your benefit as the potential buyer. Once you have given them the full retail value of the collection, and educated them on all the pieces in the collection, offer them a price that is a significant portion of the collection's overall value. By significant I mean between 50-80 percent. Paying more than 80 percent has never made sense to me as a collector. I can basically pay full retail anywhere. More times than not, you will score the collection if you follow this simple formula. Honesty truly is the best policy when it comes to life in general, and certainly when collecting the old original Hot Wheels.

CHAPTER 11

The Hunt Goes On

My passion for uncovering things is something that has been with me my entire life. A true desire that I was born with. I, to this day, enjoy browsing antique shops, flea markets, yard sales and the like, always looking for what else, old Hot Wheels. I truly believe that originality only occurs once in a collectible's lifetime, and must be preserved by passionate collectors. The history of Hot Wheels is in the hands of us, the collector community, and it is a big responsibility shared by all.

Who knows what the next 25 years of collecting will bring for me. If it's only half as good as the first 25, I'm in for one heck of a ride. For me, it's always been about the hunt. My love for Hot Wheels began as a young boy and my passion is still just as strong 50 years later. This truly speaks volumes to the beauty and ingenuity that these little toy cars possess. To be a Hot Wheels collector you must always hold on to that little kid inside of you that fell in love with the cars in the first place, and for me, it was way back in 1968. My greatest year ever!

www.RedlineArcheology.com

To contact Bob Young visit www.RedlineArcheology.com

OR

Email him: *Sportspa@comcast.net*